Captain Henry Jackson

of HMS Defiance at
WEARDE, SALTASH 1896
SHIP-TO-SHIP WIRELESS
COMMUNICATIONS PIONEER
BY JOHN HOOPER

Printed by PDS Print www.pdsprint.co.uk 01752 343491

Published by John Hooper   First Edition 2007

ISBN 978-0-9557346-0-1

Whilst every care has been taken, the Editor cannot accept responsibility for any inaccuracies. All rights reserved. No part of this publication may be reproduced or transmitted in any form or by any means, electronical or mechanical, including photocopying or recording. Nor should any part be committed to any form of data storage and retrieval system without permission from the author/publisher.

KEEP IT UNDER YOUR HAT

The hat is made of straw and in its original condition, (see page 40 with sailors in the funeral procession wearing straw hats).

In the days before modern materials, seafarers used tar to protect themselves and their belongings from the elements. Sailors were known as Jack Tars because of their clever use of this natural substance to waterproof belongings. The name Tar, in this context, dates back to the 17th century and is short for 'tarpaulin' which in those days meant a seaman. In a bid to keep dry, mariners slapped tar on hats, capes, coats and even sea chests. The hat featured above, is circa early 1900's – and is from the Author's collection.

With a sincere thank you to the Sponsors

Graham Mills, Mills Milk Alexandra Square Saltash 01752 844419

Royal Naval Amateur Radio Society (RNARS) Chairman Mr. M Puttick

21 Sandyfield Crescent Cowplain Waterlooville (G3LIK)

Sir Richard Carew-Pole

Virgin Trains Euston Station London

Colin Breed MP SE Cornwall

Nicholls & Sainsbury Solicitors 131/135 Fore Street Saltash 01752 846116

Viscountess Boyd Charitable Trust & Lord & Lady Boyd

Cottons Taxi Service Saltash 01752 848484

Carlton Plastics Kingsmill Road Saltash 01752 845805

Spinnaker International Ltd. Spinnaker House Saltash Parkway 01752 850300

Norman Tozer JP

Dr. Vincent Hooper University of New South Wales Sydney Australia

(former pupil saltash.net community school)

Taunton Security Ltd 4 Middle St Taunton 01823 335182

Mary Crawford Saltash & District Observer 01579 345699

Appleby Westward Group Ltd Moorlands Trading Estate Saltash 01752 854000

First Great Western Milford House Swindon

Streamline Protect Unit 19 Saltash Business Park 01752 848148

Castles Kitchens Ltd Estover Close Plymouth 01752 737333

Acknowledgements

Steve Johnson   www.cyberheritage.co.uk

Colin Squires & Saltash Heritage 17 Lower Fore St Saltash PL12 6JQ

Lt. Cdr. Trevor Day RN Rtd

"Arry" Harrison *saltash.net community school*

Brian Giles & Saltash Amateur Radio Club

HMS Collingwood Museum of Communications & Radar & Lt Cdr W Legg

The Churchill Archives Centre Cambridge & Claire Knight

"Ritchie" Richardson MBE Saltash

Ditton Park Archives & Rutherford Appleton Laboratory & Sarah James

Jackson's letter reproduced with the permission of Curtis Brown Ltd on behalf of The Estate of Winston Churchill

Lt. Norman Ash RN Rtd

Bruce Hunt Saltash

Barratts Photo Press photograph of Admiral Jackson & his Wife

Norma Cabble for artwork

Patricia Haskins Burraton Coombe Saltash

Richard Paynter Saltash

Phyllis Crawford Forder Saltash

A special thank you to Colin Squires for his tireless and thorough editing of this book.

FOREWORD

As Headteacher of saltash.net community school, I feel honoured to have been invited to write the foreword to this fascinating book about the history of Wearde Quay.

Three years ago, we became a specialist school in Science and Mathematics and Computing. At the launch of our specialism, John Hooper, and his wife, Sue, who was Mayor of Saltash at that time, spoke with me about the very special significance of our chosen specialism. They shared with me the fact that the first ship-to-ship wireless communication in the world had taken place just below our school site in 1896.

One hundred and eight years later, in 2004, we had just installed a wireless network at our school to enable all our staff and students to have access to the internet from anywhere on the site. We thought we were being innovative! But as I spoke further with John and Sue I put our developments in the context of those 19th Century pioneers, like Jackson and Marconi, who paved the way for the amazing technological advances of the 20th and 21st Centuries.

This book, and the history it charts, will be an inspiration to all learners, young and old. Jackson's work reflects so well the words of an unknown but astute philosopher, who once said,

> "Let us not follow where existing paths lead, but go instead where there is no path and leave a trail for others to follow."

I thank John for all the hard work and effort which has gone into the compilation of this book. I have no doubt that it will be an invaluable resource for our local area and for further afield, for anyone who seeks a greater understanding of how the past impacts upon the present.

Isobel Bryce
October 2007

Preface

My book on Captain Henry Jackson (later Admiral Jackson) the Saltash based famous Ships' Communications Pioneer; And, indeed, featuring the way of life around Wearde Quay, the River Lynher and the Hamoaze - came about as a result of one of our regular visits to the school, as consort to my wife, who was Mayor of Saltash (Councillor Sue Hooper MBE) at the time.

saltash.net community school had been celebrating its Special School status in Science and Mathematics and Computing, and as a result, had developed its Communications Technology and IT Department, which directly overlooks the site at Wearde Quay, Saltash, where the Torpedo Training Ship HMS DEFIANCE was based, and where Captain Henry Jackson developed and transmitted the very first Ship-to-Ship wireless communications in 1896.

To mark the 110th Anniversary of this amazing pioneering feat, it was suggested, that as I had presented the School with a portfolio of the historic details with supporting rare photographs and documentation, that I should consider writing a book, where the proceeds would benefit the School. It seemed fitting, that given the School's special status, which coincided with the 110th Anniversary, that this important record be published to benefit the School.

I would like to thank in particular Steve Johnson, Cyberheritage, for allowing me to use his rare photographs and information, which I have gratefully acknowledged in my book.

Our local Heritage Centre, Colin Squires and Saltash Amateur Radio Club, have supported the production of the book, together with the Naval History Museum in HMS Collingwood, Fareham, which has kindly allowed me to use some of its photographs and information. My sincere appreciation is also conveyed to my many sponsors.

I would wish to thank my wife Sue for her unstinting work and support through-out the long process of the book. Also, Norman Tozer JP for his administrative support.

For me, writing this book has been an exciting journey back in time, and I have enjoyed it immensely. I hope you, the reader, will enjoy your historic voyage too!

John. W. Hooper
(Author.)

Yet my 'great-grandfather'
was but a water-man,
looking one way, and rowing another:
and I got most of my estate by the same occupation.

The Pilgrims Progress
John Bunyan 1628-88

This crew is rowing back to base – HMS DEFIANCE –
Where my story begins – Read on!!!!

Dedicated to
Florence Hope
and
Rose Elizabeth Grace

COMMANDING OFFICER CAPTAIN HENRY JACKSON HMS DEFIANCE

HMS Defiance was a Royal Naval Torpedo School close to Saltash. It enjoyed early prosperity due to its proximity to Devonport Dockyard, or Dock as it was initially called. The outrigger torpedoes were in their infancy and could only be aimed at the target if the boat was pointing in the same direction and towards the target area.

On the floating hulks that made up the school, and ashore, mines and torpedoes were prepared and techniques taught, how magnetism and electrics operated in warfare. Over the years thousands of men passed through Defiance at Wearde Quay and Wilcove. If you visit the localities you can almost hear their laughter, cheers and curses. The very presence of the 'Defiance' establishment would have given the area a buzz.

Part of the curriculum of the school was the firing of live explosive submarine mines and Whitehead Torpedoes. These were fired up the River Lynher and in the official range in Cawsand Bay. The Whitehead torpedo was invented by Robert Whitehead born in Bolton 1823, and in 1866 he developed a floating torpedo which could hit a target at about 700 yards and at a speed of seven knots after being fired underwater by compressed air. He was living in Trieste which was a part of the Austro-Hungarian Empire in 1867, having moved from Milan due to unrest. It was in 1850 that he had been approached by the Austrian Navy to produce a new weapon.

Admiral Sir Henry Bradwardine Jackson

Among his numerous honours were K.C.V.O (1906), the K.C.B (1910) and the G.C.B. (1916). He also received honorary degrees from Oxford, Cambridge and Leeds Universities. Foreign honours included Grand Cross of the Spanish Order of Naval Merit in 1909, The Japanese Order of the Rising Sun, and the Russian Order of the White Eagle. He was also a grand Officer of the Legion of Honour. For his scientific expertise, he was made Honorary Vice-President of the Institution of Naval Architects

1855 21 Dec	Born in Barnsley into a family whose lineage can be traced back to Sir Jno Jackson, Knight of Edwardthorpe (now Edderthorpe) Darfield and Hickleton; c 1580.
1861	Was educated at home by a governess. Later educated at Chester and at Stubbington House, Fareham.
1868 Dec	Joined the Royal Navy at the age of 13.
1878/79	Junior Lieutenant on board HMS Active on the African Station. Participated in the Zulu Wars.
1881	Lieutenant on board the Agincourt.
1881	Appointed to HMS Vernon, Torpedo School Ship at Portsmouth.
1890 Jan	Promoted to Commander.
1895	In command of the Torpedo School Training Ship HMS Defiance at Wearde Quay Saltash Cornwall.
1896 Jun	Promoted to the rank of Captain.
1897	Appointed Naval attaché in Paris.
1899	Appointed Commander of the Torpedo Depot Ship HMS Vulcan.
1901	Elected as a fellow of the Royal Society in recognition of his work in the field of Wireless Telegraphy.
1902	Appointed Assistant Director of Torpedoes at the Admiralty.
1903	Captain of HMS Vernon.
1905	Appointed Third Sea Lord and Controller of the Navy.
1908	Appointed to command the Third (afterwards known as the Sixth) Cruiser Squadron in the Mediterranean.
1910	Represented the Admiralty at the International Conference on Aerial Navigation in Paris.
1911	Assumed the direction of the newly created Royal Navy War College at Portsmouth, training the First World War Staff Officers.
1913	Appointed Chief of the War Staff at the Admiralty.
1914 War	Nominated as Commander in Chief, Mediterranean, but instead of taking over that command, he was retained at the Admiralty.
1915 May	Selected to succeed Lord Fisher as First Sea Lord.
1916 Dec	Appointed President of the Royal Naval College at Greenwich.
1919 Jul	Advanced to the rank of Admiral of the Fleet.
1917 -1919	Served as Principal Naval Aide-de Camp to King George V.
1924 Jul	Retired from the Royal Navy.
1929 July	Died at his home, Salterns House, Hayling Island. Buried in the neighbouring Churchyard. Memorial Service held in Westminster Abbey.

Admiral Sir Henry Bradwardine Jackson Passed away at his home Salterns House, Hayling Island and was buried in the neighbouring St Mary's Churchyard. There was a memorial service in Westminster Abbey.

PHOTO PATRICIA DAY, SALTASH

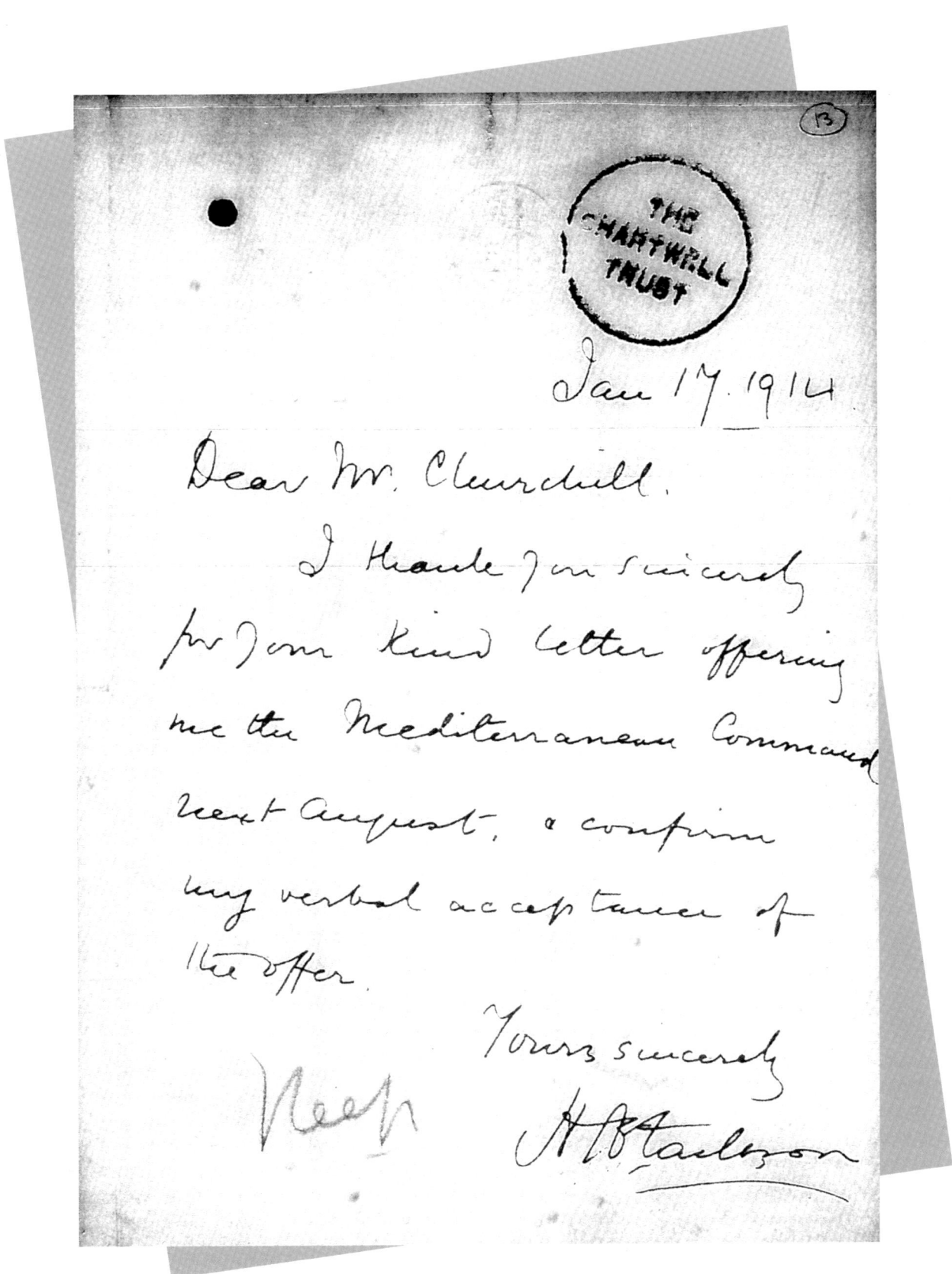

A copy of a letter by Henry Jackson replying to Winston Churchill in 1914 accepting the position as Commander in Chief, Mediterranean

IMAGE© THE WINSTON CHURCHILL ARCHIVE TRUST

ROYAL NAVAL ENGINEERING COLLEGE PHOTOGRAPHIC CLUB KEYHAM 1891

This is a photo of the Photographic Club at the Royal Naval Engineering College, Keyham, in 1891. Some photographs in the book have remained unseen for many years in an old photograph album. All taken by one man, believed to be a Petty Officer in the Royal Navy, they provide what may be a unique insight into the day-to-day workings of the British Royal Navy, from the sole viewpoint of one individual. The photographer could be the one seated, hands clasped, and second from left. How I would like to know his name? Did any of the above photographers with their cumbersome equipment eventually capture the images of war?

Steve Johnson Cyberheritage

THE CREW OF HMS DEFIANCE

In the above photograph taken on board the former HMS Flamingo is the ship's crew of Defiance, which consisted mainly of seamen training for the rating of torpedo men. On board there would have been a number of retired sailors employed mainly for general help, cleaning and assistance.

The lower image is a group of officers, Captain Jackson is the officer seated to the right of the centre and can be recognised by the lace on the peak of his cap. The officer to his right is Lieutenant Orpen, the First Lieutenant. The personnel seated in the front are Warrant Officers with the exception of the one on the right who is the head schoolmaster. The photograph was taken on the upper deck of the Defiance.

Courtesy Steve Johnson, Cyberheritage

Henry Jackson and HMS Defiance, Wearde Quay

Near the end of the 19th century, a remarkable achievement by a great man took place in the Lynher estuary, near Saltash. It was the first of two historic events in the development of radio communication that occurred in the County of Cornwall. (The transmission of transatlantic signals from Poldhu, near Mullion, masterminded by Guglielmo Marconi in 1901, was the second.)

In the Lynher the experimenter was Capt. Henry Jackson R.N. operating on board HMS Defiance, which was attached to the Devonport naval base. The circumstances are described below.

HMS Defiance (the 12th British Navy ship to bear the name), a 5,000 tons warship, was built at Pembroke Dock in Wales. When completed in 1861, the advent of ironclad ships meant that she was already obsolete, so she was never armed. In the early 1880s, the Admiralty decided that Devonport should have its own torpedo-training establishment (Portsmouth already had HMS Vernon). Accordingly Defiance was converted into a 'school-ship'. She was commissioned in December 1884 but remained at the Dockyard while the instructional facilities were worked up.

Early in 1886 Defiance was towed into the Lynher and permanently moored on the north side of the deep-water channel, off Wearde Quay. To the west, a mine-laying practice area and a torpedo range were laid out. Various vessels were assigned to Defiance to act as tenders, bringing stores and personnel from the Dockyard. Pinnaces and other small boats were provided for journeys around the practice areas and across to Wearde Quay.

Over the years, other hulks were added to increase the extent of the training and the accommodation; footbridges linked them. (Officially, these vessels lost their original names and became part of 'HMS Defiance'.) By 1892 the total complement plus trainees exceeded 500; by 1920 the figure had reached 1,000. Better transport was needed, so in 1905 Defiance Halt was created on the main railway line above Wearde Quay, and arrangements were made for the Great Western Railway's Plymouth–Saltash suburban service (started the previous year) to be extended to it.

Various sporting facilities were provided onshore; these were expanded in 1924 when the Admiralty rented a field at St Stephens for use as a recreation ground.

By 1930 the principal vessel (the original Defiance) was nearly 70 years old and her wooden hull was beginning to decay, so a replacement had to be found. The vessel chosen was an 11,000-ton cruiser, but her 25-feet draught meant that she required a deeper berth than existed off Wearde Quay at low water. Thus the Admiralty decided to close down the Wearde Quay establishment and relocate the training base at an anchorage in the Hamoaze, just north of Wilcove (it had recently been vacated by the HMS Indus artificers' training school). In the Lynher, only the practice areas were retained.

So on 13th October 1930, Defiance was towed away by tugs, ending almost 45 years of service at Wearde Quay. During those years HMS Defiance had become part of the business, social and sporting life of St Stephens and Saltash.

Henry Bradwardine Jackson was born in Yorkshire in 1855; his father was a solicitor. He joined the Royal Navy as a cadet just before his 14th birthday, and was trained on HMS Britannia, Dartmouth (still a <u>ship</u> at that time). By 1878 he had reached the rank of Lieutenant, and in 1881 was posted to HMS Vernon, the torpedo-school ship at Portsmouth. All things technical had always fascinated him, and on Vernon he became intensely interested in the electrics of torpedoes.

Jackson was also aware that the Royal Navy had a growing problem regarding signalling. This had become obvious during annual manoeuvres in the late 1880s, in one of which Jackson had commanded a torpedo boat. The main task of torpedo boats was to attack, or act as guard-boats, in groups at night. For night-time identification they relied on different coloured lights, or lamps sending Morse Code – not at all satisfactory.

In 1887 Henry Jackson got engaged to Alice Burbury, daughter of Samuel Burbury, a prominent mathematician who was publishing work on electromagnetic theory at that time. Henry and Alice were married in 1890, the same year that he was promoted to the rank of Commander and posted to the battleship HMS Edinburgh to be second-in-command. During the next few years Jackson began to consider a possible use for 'Hertzian waves' (as radio waves were then called) to overcome the ship identification problem, and also got some advice from his father-in-law.

For most of 1894 Jackson was at HMS Vernon, Portsmouth, as a member of a committee considering new torpedo designs. Then in January 1895 he was posted to HMS Defiance to take command of the establishment. Once he had settled in, Jackson turned his attention to radio waves again. He constructed a transmitter and a receiver, and began experimenting on board the ship. He had some success, particularly in designing aerials.

During the period of his posting to HMS Defiance, January 1895 – October 1897, Henry and Alice Jackson lived at Boisdale House, North Road, Saltash (now a residential home). The house was let to a succession of naval officers in the late 19th and early 20th centuries. Jackson was promoted to the rank of Captain in June 1896.

At a War Office conference held on 31st August 1896, Jackson met the young Guglielmo Marconi for the first time. On that occasion and at subsequent meetings they exchanged details of their equipment and the results they had achieved. Despite their 20-year age difference, they struck up a lasting friendship.

The transmission distances achieved by Jackson as he made successive improvements to his equipment and aerials can be summarized as follows.

August 1896	from one end of HMS Defiance to the other,
Autumn 1896	300 yards, from a tender back to Defiance,
Winter 1896-7	1,200 yards, with the transmitter aboard the gunboat HMS Scourge, one of Defiance's tenders,
Spring 1897	signals could be received from Scourge wherever she went in the estuaries, whether it was 2 miles up the Lynher (she was too big to go further) or 3 miles down the Hamoaze at Cremyll.

Thus the first ever ship-to-ship radio communication took place in the Lynher estuary. All Marconi's work had been done on land – he didn't install a radio set in a ship until July 1897.

In October 1897, Jackson set up a radio link for everyday use between HMS Defiance and the Port Admiral's House at Mount Wise, Devonport. That was his last piece of practical radio work for some time, because on 1st November he was posted to Paris to become Naval Attaché to the British Embassy there.

Henry Jackson took part in the Royal Navy's Summer Manoeuvres of 1899.

For the first time, radio was to be used during that event, and three ships were equipped. One of them was HMS Juno, a light cruiser. She was under the command of Capt. Jackson, and Marconi was on board as an observer. The successful results of the radio operations on that occasion led to the installation of wireless telegraphy (as radio was then called) in many of the Royal Navy's ships. By the end of 1900, the Navy had 51 radio sets – 32 designed by Marconi and 19 designed by Jackson. In 1901 a further 52 sets were manufactured at HMS Vernon after Jackson had vetted an improved version of his design.

Subsequently Jackson received regular promotions: Rear Admiral in 1906, Vice-Admiral in 1911, and full Admiral in 1914. Jackson was also held in very high regard in the scientific world. He was honoured by being elected to a Fellowship of the Royal Society in 1901. He received a knighthood in 1906, and another knighthood in 1910 – the first was of the Royal Victorian Order, the second was of the Order of the Bath.

In 1915, Sir John Fisher, who had been First Sea Lord since 1904, resigned. ('Jacky' Fisher) was the man who prepared the British Navy for the Great War.) Admiral Sir Henry Jackson was then made First Sea Lord. He was well suited to the post, being an excellent all-rounder, not just a radio expert. However, at that time Germany's ruthless campaign of submarine warfare was growing steadily. The Royal Navy's efforts to combat it were not successful, and the destruction of our merchant shipping continued to increase. Jackson had to 'carry the can', and in December 1916 he was replaced as First Sea Lord by Admiral Jellicoe.

Jackson was then appointed President of the Royal Naval College at Greenwich, a post that he filled with great distinction until 1919, when he was advanced to the rank of Admiral of the Fleet. In 1920 he was appointed the first chairman of the government's Radio Research Board.

After he had completed his active naval service, Jackson was able to spend time at home on his favourite pursuit – experimenting with radio and electronics. He also participated fully in the activities of the Royal Society and the Institution of Electrical Engineers.

Admiral Sir Henry Jackson, GCB, KCVO, FRS, DSc, LLD, MIEE, died at his home on Hayling Island, near Portsmouth, on 14th December 1929. He was 74. His grave is in St Mary's Churchyard, South Hayling.

To sum up, in 1896 Henry Jackson was:

the first Briton to use radio waves for practical communication,

the first person anywhere in the world to achieve ship-to-ship radio communication,

and he accomplished these deeds in Cornwall, off Wearde Quay in the Lynher estuary,

while he was a resident of Saltash.

Clearly, Jackson was the 'father' of Maritime Radio – a resource that had a great and lasting impact on safety at sea.

Colin Squires October 2007

HERTZIAN WAVES

Captain Jackson first had the idea of using Hertzian waves for naval signalling when he was the Commander of HMS Edinburgh in 1893, but it was not until 1895, after he had been experimenting directly from the writings of Hertz and Lodge that he read some work by Dr. Bose on the properties of coherers of which he had been unaware.

He was then a Captain, and in command of the Torpedo Training School HMS Defiance which was moored at Wearde Quay in the River Lynher below where the saltash.net community school is sited. By early 1896 he had evolved a successful transmitter and receiver, the details of which can be seen on the photographs (with permission of the Museum in HMS Collingwood). This was the first wireless telegraphy equipment to be fitted in a naval ship and trials with HMS Scourge resulted in the transmission of messages successfully over 5,800 yards and at 10 words a minute.

The experiments continued through 1897, during which time some of the fundamental laws governing these techniques were realised, and some of the drawbacks of the equipment used made themselves felt. The main problem was the vulnerability of the induction coil to dampness, and Captain Jackson pointed out in a report:

"That it is possible to construct and enclose a coil that will work efficiently in all conditions of atmospheric dampness there is no doubt, but it being a new point to require from the manufacturers, it necessarily takes some time to get them to move in the matter, unless at very great expense."

All Captain Jackson's earlier work had been without any knowledge of Marconi's. In September 1896, he met Marconi at the War Office, and thereafter both men corresponded and exchanged information. Each man's apparatus was remarkably similar, but Marconi's had the benefit of rather more development and showed slightly better results. By 1899, a fairly reliable version of the Jackson (or 'Service' set as it became known) was fitted in a number of ships, and it continued as a competitor to the Marconi equipment for some years. Jackson himself reported on comparative trials of his own and Marconi's sets fitted in the Fleet that, generally, the Marconi sets were more sensitive but 'Service' sets more easily maintained and to set up, and more reliable. Later in the Mediterranean, he concentrated on developing a tuned system, which he realised, was both effective and possibly more secure. The term used to describe this development was 'Syntony' – syntonic W/T (wireless transmitter). The 'Jiggers' or tuning coils became one of the main features of all W/T equipment at the time.

Between them Captain Henry Jackson and Guglielmo Marconi persuaded the Admiralty to carry out trials during the Fleet manoeuvres of 1899 in the Channel. Marconi fitted his sets to four ships, one of them, HMS Juno being commanded by Captain Jackson. Ranges of 60 to 70 miles were achieved and the Admiralty were suitably impressed. In 1900, during the war in South Africa three Marconi sets were fitted to cruisers on blockade duties, and later that year the Admiralty purchased 32 Marconi sets for afloat and ashore. In 1901 a further fifty 'Service' sets were ordered for use within the Fleets. By the time the hostilities commenced with Germany in 1914, the majority of ships in the Royal Navy were equipped with one or two wireless sets.

In 1903, the standard set in use in the Fleet was the 'Service' set, which consisted of an amalgam of the Jackson and Marconi components modified by the use of a silenced spark gap and a magnetic detector.

THE TRANSMITTER

Captain Henry Jackson RN designed the Jackson sending and receiving apparatus of 1896. It was used, with success, to send and receive messages in Morse code at a speed of 10 W.P.M. between HMS Defiance and HMS Scourge in the River Lynher and the Plymouth Waters.

The transmitter equipment consisted of an induction coil with a key to make and break the supply to the primary winding. The secondary winding was attached to the two outside members of the four brass balls forming a Hertz oscillator. The bottom brass ball was earthed, and the top ball was connected to the aerial.

Pressing the key allowed current to flow in the primary winding, inducing a voltage in the secondary winding, which caused a spark to jump between the four brass balls of the oscillator, resulting in electromagnetic waves radiating from the aerial.

THE RECEIVER

On the receiver, when the electromagnetic waves cut the receiving aerial an EMF (Electro-Magnetic-Field) was induced in it. The resistance of 'glass tube', to which the aerial was attached, was lowered, allowing a small single cell battery to operate a relay. When the single contact of this relay closed, current flowed from a local six-cell battery through the coils of a vibrator. The moving arm of the vibrator performed two functions; it completed the circuit to the sounder or 'inker', and physically tapped the 'glass tube', restoring its high resistance. This stopped the current from the single cell and broke the relay contact, thus returning the whole circuit to its original condition. Hence a 'long' in Morse code would have appeared as a prolonged number of movements of the vibrator arm, in sympathy with the fluctuating EMF in the aerial.

ADMIRAL JACKSON WITH HIS WIFE

In 1920 the Radio Research Board of the Department of Scientific and Industrial Research was formed with the Admiral of the Fleet, Henry Jackson as the Board's first Chair. Four sub-committees were established on *propagation, atmospherics, direction finding and thermionic valves.* Early members included E.V.Appleton, R.L. Smith-Rose and R.A.Watson-Watt.

Atmospheric research was undertaken at the Aldershot Wireless Station and direction finding work began in the West Park of the Compass Observatory at Ditton Park, Slough.

Under Henry Jackson's guidance, and in his presence, important experiments were carried out with propagation of wireless waves and the nature of atmospherics, radio direction finding and precise radio frequency measurements. More than 100 important papers were published. In 1926 the Royal Society presented him with his most prized award, the Hughes Medal.

It is to say with no exaggeration that British prestige in the scientific world of radio telegraphy owes so much to Admiral Henry Jackson.

Photo Ditton Park Archives & Rutherton Appleton Laboratory

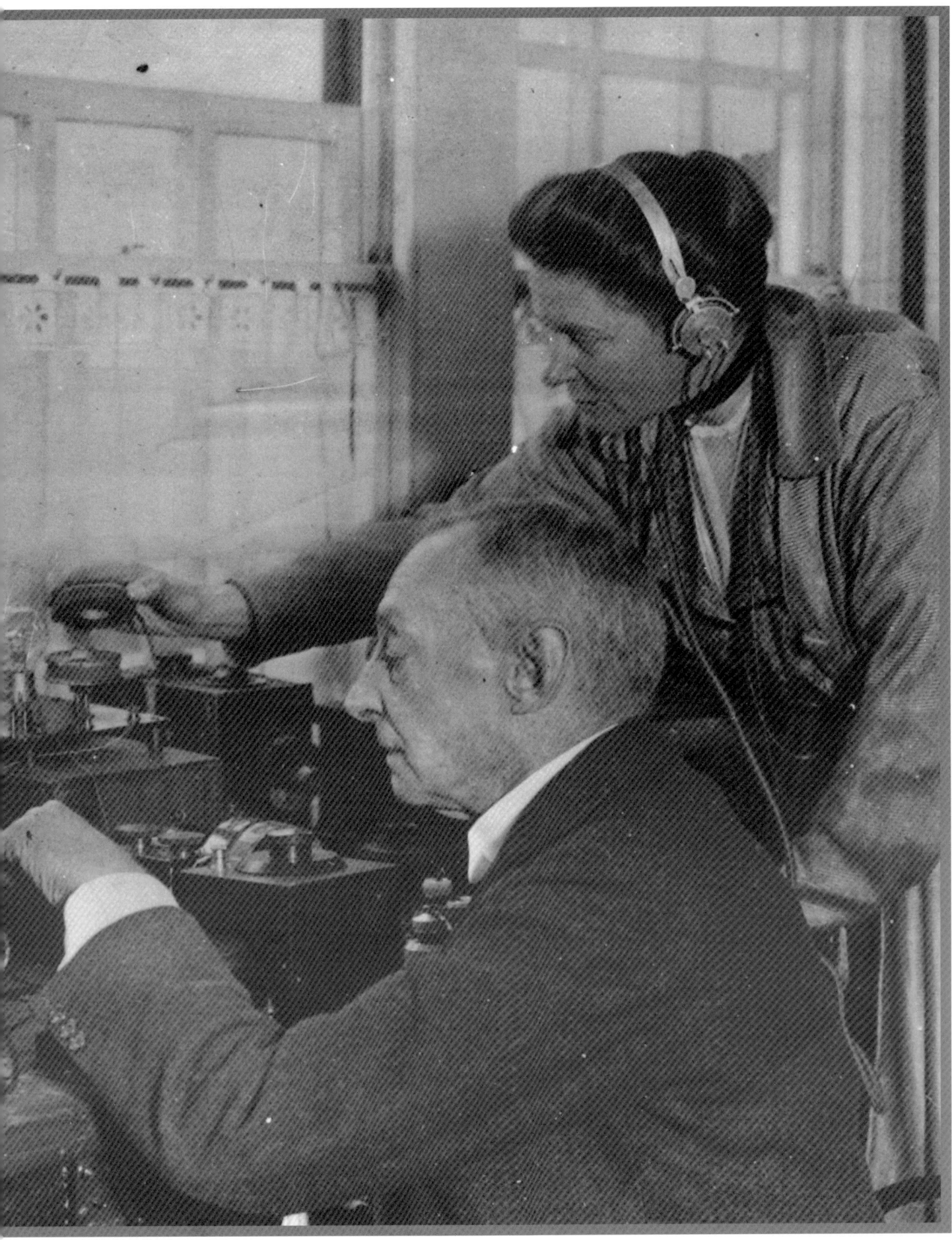

In the latter part of the 19th Century and early 20th Century Henry Jackson's contemporaries, the Russian Popov and the Italian Marconi were also experimenting with wireless communications.

ALEXANDER STEPANOVICH POPOV

In Russia, Popov is regarded as the inventor of radio communication, though in the rest of the world, the Italian Guglielmo Marconi is generally recognised to have been the first to demonstrate the practical application of electromagnetic waves. As with Henry Bradwardine Jackson, Popov was required to sign a nondisclosure statement because he taught at the Marine Engineering School, part of the Russian navy. In 1896, Marconi applied for a patent for his wireless work, which gained him the credit for the invention of radio.

In the year before Marconi's patent application, Popov had expanded on earlier work in electromagnetism done by Henry Hertz and Oliver Lodge. On 7th May 1895, Popov demonstrated a wireless receiver consisting of a metal 'coherer'—a device that detects electromagnetic waves—an antenna, a relay, and a bell to signal the presence of these waves. Popov could send and then detect them up to 64 metres away. Although not initially intended as a means of transmitting information, Popov's device proved that radio communication was feasible. Initially Popov was trying to detect thunderstorms in advance by picking up static electrical signals which led him to experiment with wireless.

Every year, Russians celebrate Popov's successful demonstration of wireless transmission on 7th May—so-called Radio Day, which was established in 1945.

A National hero in Russia, Popov came from simple beginnings, the son of a Priest, he grew up in the Turinsk mining district of Russia in the Ural Mountains. He studied engineering at the University of St. Petersburg. After graduation, he joined the Russian Navy's Torpedo School and later the Marine Engineering School as an instructor. In 1901, Popov was named director of the Electro Technical Institute in St. Petersburg.

In 1905 he became seriously ill, after being very uneasy about the suppression of a student movement. He died of a brain haemorrhage aged 47 on 31st December 1905, which corresponds to 13th January, 1906 in the Gregorian calendar.

GUGLIELMO MARCONI

When Marconi began experimenting in 1894, radio waves were known as 'Hertzian Waves'. A few years earlier Heinrich Hertz had produced and detected the waves across his laboratory. Marconi's achievement was to produce and detect the waves over long distances, laying the foundations for what today we know as radio. The family home was his Italian father's villa near Bologna. His mother who was Irish often took Guglielmo to visit relatives in England. When Marconi was home in Bologna their neighbour, the distinguished physicist Professor Righi, interested the young Guglielmo in electricity generally and the works of Hertz. Marconi repeated Hertz's experiments in the family home. Hertzian waves were produced by sparks in one circuit and detected in another circuit a few metres away. Marconi could soon detect signals over several kilometres and this led him to try and interest the Italian Ministry of Posts and Telegraphs.

He was unsuccessful, but in 1896 his cousin, Henry Jameson-Davis, introduced him to William Preece, Engineer-in-Chief of the British Post Office. Encouraging demonstrations in London and on Salisbury Plain followed and in 1897 Marconi obtained a patent and established the Wireless Telegraph and Signal Company Limited, which opened the world's first radio factory at Chelmsford, England in 1898. Experiments and demonstrations continued. Queen Victoria at Osborne House received bulletins by radio about the health of the Prince of Wales, convalescent on the Royal Yacht off Cowes. In 1901 signals were received across the Atlantic. Broadcasting as we know it was still in the future - the BBC was established in 1922 - but Marconi had achieved his aim of turning Hertz's laboratory demonstration into a practical means of communication.

At 12.30 a.m. on the 12th of December 1901, in St. John's Newfoundland, Marconi distinguished three faint clicks through the earphones of his wireless receiver -- the Morse code letter 'S' and a new discovery was born. The signal was sent from the Poldhu Wireless Station located on a cliff along the Lizard coast of Cornwall, where the base of the 1900-33 station can be seen with a commemorative obelisk.

Marconi won the Nobel Prize for Physics in 1909. He was born 25th April 1874 and died 20th July 1937 (aged 63) in Rome.

OTHER CORNWALL BASED COMPETETIVE RADIO AND WIRELESS PIONEERS

It is noteworthy that there were many early telecommunications providers in the 19th and 20th Centuries, providing services in Countries around the Globe. Cable and Wireless was a leading Company working from Porthcurno in Cornwall.

Unfortunately, space does not allow the author to greatly elaborate; however, at the same time as Marconi was experimenting, and successfully sending signals from Poldhu to Newfoundland in 1901, Cable and Wireless Companies (Pender Group, part of the Anglo-American Telegraph Company), were closely watching, and serious disagreements and confrontations developed. Indeed, the Group had been around a long time, and had the monopoly of communications in Newfoundland and were opposed to any further experiments. This greatly annoyed Marconi, so he moved his work to Nova Scotia, where he found the Americans and Canadians more receptive to his work and achievements.

However, the Pender Group of Companies were still concerned about Marconi's exploits and had a mast secretly installed in its Cornwall Station and listened in on Marconi's experiments, and at least, on one occasion disrupted a demonstration of wireless transmission.

Eventually, both stakeholders felt it was more advantageous to work together in the name of progress (profits too I suspect), and on 8th April 1929 they merged Companies.

FOOTNOTE – *It is interesting to note that a former Mayor of Saltash, Mona Tomaszewska-Honywill (nee Nancarrow), recalls her uncle (Arthur Nancarrow), working at the Radio Station at Porthcurno in the early 1900's, and has some wonderful recollections and interesting memorabilia. Unfortunately, Arthur died untimely, at the age of 25 years in 1911 in St Vincent, Windward Isles, whilst in the employment of The Western Telegraph Company Limited. When he was 10 years of age he was attending Longlands School not far from his home in Burraton Coombe. His first overseas appointment was in Madeira with a salary of £72 per annum, he also worked in Rio de Janeiro for 22 months and his salary had risen to £120 per annum.*

The Poldhu site in Cornwall was chosen for its remoteness to keep the project away from the media and the public. (Marconi eventually set up sites in Cape Cod, Massachusetts, and in Glace Bay, Canada). It was in 1900 that Marconi worked in secret without the press hounding him or speculating on the outcome of his experiments. He was only 27 years old at the time and would not be dissuaded by critics, including many scientists who were convinced that the curvature of the earth would prevent wireless waves travelling in a straight line. Indeed, Marconi did experience a set- back in 1901 when the 200 feet masts were blown down in a storm but a temporary aerial was erected, and eventually replaced with a more sturdy structure of four wooden towers.

Sadly the Poldhu Wireless Station was dismantled in 1933, four years before the death of Guglielmo Marconi. Almost 70 years on, a new Marconi Centre, at Poldhu, started as a dream for 21st Century enthusiasts. On 12th December, 2001 that dream became a reality when the keys were handed over to the Poldhu Amateur Radio Club (PARC). It was Carolyn Rule, the chairperson of the Radio Club whose idea it was for a new centre. The centre will now act as a home for PARC and as a lasting tribute, and fitting memorial to Marconi's work.

Lady Mary Holborrow, the Lord Lieutenant of Cornwall attended the opening ceremony representing the Queen. She sent a message to Canada from the new Centre at Poldhu, at exactly four pm, she also sent a message in Morse code to Signal Hill in Canada; It was timed to the second to coincide with the Centenary of Marconi's transmission in 1901. In a nearby field, next to the remains of the original building Marconi had used - his Grandson Guglielmo Marconi who likewise, was in Poldhu to celebrate his Grandfather's achievements, also performed a similar experiment when he sent a message to Canada, using a spark gap transmitter just like his Grandfather had done in 1901.

Kevin Hale, John Bailey, Lt. Cdr Trevor Day, Sue Hooper, Kevin McKane, Tony Beddington Brian Giles, John Hooper, Bert Lee.

CENTENARY OF HENRY JACKSON'S RADIO EXPERIMENTS

On the Saturday, 31st August 1996 Saltash Amateur Radio Club set up a radio station below Saltash Community School, perhaps in the same place that the Defiance crews rolled the grass and had their football and cricket days with all kinds of sports to keep the men fit and healthy.

The radio was set up to commemorate the Centenary of Henry Jackson's pioneering radio experiments from the two wooden hulks in the Lynher.

On the day the Mayor of Saltash Sue Hooper and her Consort (yours truly) visited the station and we were welcomed by the President Roland Hewett, Chairman Kevin McKane, and the Chairman of RNARS, Lt Commander Trevor Day.

Insets:
The Mayor making a transmission on the day from the station set up at Wearde.

The Mayor spoke to a radio amateur in Farnborough who had trained on HMS Defiance many years ago.

The station was set up with three transmitters that were active from Thursday evening to Sunday afternoon in perfect weather conditions. There were several aerials and caravans housed the equipment for transmitting. The locations are known as 'shacks' whether it is a house or a field.

During the three days 399 contacts where made including Ontario and Israel, a canal boat on the Gloucester canal, and a yacht off Fowey. Other interesting contacts came from HMS Belfast in the Pool of London, a Royal Air Force museum at Duxford in Cambridge, an air display at Shoreham and the Royal Signals at Colerne near Bath; two hundred stations were contacted in the United Kingdom and other countries contacted included the Ukraine, Estonia, Italy and France; contacts could be heard in Japan, Fiji and Taiwan but the beam was not strong enough for the club members to talk to them. There were 12 members on duty most of the weekend and a lot of others who visited the 'shack'.

Courtesy Saltash Amateur Radio Club

THE DEFIANCE AFLOAT

PHOTO'S COURTESY STEVE JOHNSON CYBERHERITAGE

Views from the shore known today as Wearde Quay with the signal box and naval ships in the distance.

H.M.S. "DEFIANCE", SALTASH.

AUTHOR'S COLLECTION

DISCIPLINARY PROCEDURES

For many years Britain's 'Senior Service' relied upon the cane and birch to discipline its boy entrants, with both ratings and officer cadets being subject to corporal punishment. For example, at Osborne Naval College on the Isle of Wight the captain-in-charge could order the infliction of 'official cuts', laid on by a petty officer. Regulations permitted up to 12 strokes of the cane to be administered 'on the breech with clothes on.'

Until the early 1900s naval cadets were also subject to the birch, the punishment invariably being carried out in public. The procedure was described in the pages of *'The Humanitarian'*.

Read this brief memoir of the caning of officer cadets at Dartmouth Royal Naval College.

The offender is strapped hand and foot, in this case, over the bitts or the breech of a small gun, his trousers are allowed to fall below the knees, a broad canvas band is passed round the middle of his body, and his clothing is strapped up by this means, leaving thighs and buttocks uncovered. The same preliminaries are gone through as in caning, but the strokes are deliberately delivered on the bare flesh, not in rapid succession, but with a slight pause between each stroke, making the torture and agony of as lengthy a duration as possible. With each stroke the flesh is seen to turn red, blue, and black, with bruising; after six or eight strokes the skin usually breaks. At the twelfth stroke a halt is called, and a replacement corporal with a new birch supersedes the first, and the boy is allowed to drink water, which is always provided. The officer orders, 'Carry on the punishment', and the second instalment is laid on; splinters of broken birch whizz and fly in all directions and the offender often swoons, and has to be supplied with restoratives before he can be half led, half carried, to the sick berth below.

Many Naval Officers considered corporal punishment to be essential if order was to be maintained amongst their younger charges. A Vice Admiral put the point in his memoirs:

The best, and to my mind the most suitable, punishment for a boy is to cane him. It is quickly over, it does not stop his recreation, and if it hurts him sufficiently at the time, he does not

Up before the Captain's table. Defaulters?

want to have it again. I always had boys examined medically before being caned, and the caning was done in the presence of a medical officer and in private, as I do not believe in public caning.

Caning boys in Naval Training Establishments, such as the shore-based 'HMS Ganges' continued into the 1960s and 1970s. An ex-boy sailor later recalled one such punishment:

I was caught doing something which if I had been in the navy proper would have got me 'cells'. I was brought before the captain of the training ship and sentenced to 12 cuts of the cane. I was taken at once to the sickbay and told to strip off except for my socks and was given a pair of white duck punishment trousers. These are always worn by a boy who is to be caned. Then I was marched into the gym where the Master-at-Arms checked to see that I hadn't sneaked in any padding. I was told to stand to attention and the Surgeon General came in with the Regulating Petty Officer, who is always deputed to give the cuts and was carrying two long canes.

I was made to lay over the end of the gym horse and held in position by two well-built boy ratings. The Captain came in and said 'Carry on' and the RPO lifted the cane in a wide semi-circle to the back of his head and brought it down with considerable force. After each stroke the Master-at-Arms called out 'Cut delivered sir.' At the end of the 12 cuts I was taken to the sickbay my injuries were inspected. The marks had already turned a mauve-blue in colour.

Mines stored on one of the 'hulks'.

A mine explodes in the Hamoaze; fish in abundance probably stunned by the explosions would scatter the surface.

Below: Heaving in practise mines, an officer overseeing the operation.

BEREHAVEN MINE

The photographs show a party of sailors qualifying for the rating of torpedo men on the former HMS Perseus. Above: They are fitting a 'Berehaven' boat mine, so called for being used in Berehaven, Ireland, on annual manoeuvres. The cask was fitted with a small electric battery and an automatic firing arrangement. These would float on the surface attached to a plank with the charge hanging below. The mines were placed to guard against the approach of enemy during anchorage.

GUN COTTON MINE

Sailors fitting a 72lb gun cotton mine to be automatically fired on a ship striking it, but in this case the electrical battery would be on shore nearby and connected by a cable to the mine. They are called electro-contact mines.

Training session or preparing for live firing

Photo W M Crockett Plymouth

Below: Torpedo ready for firing. Preparing a 'Baby' for exercise, an 18in Baby, RGF (Royal Gun Factory) The man in white is adjusting the depth it shall run at. The next man oils the engines whilst the fins are turned and the man in the oilskin leggings is setting the range.

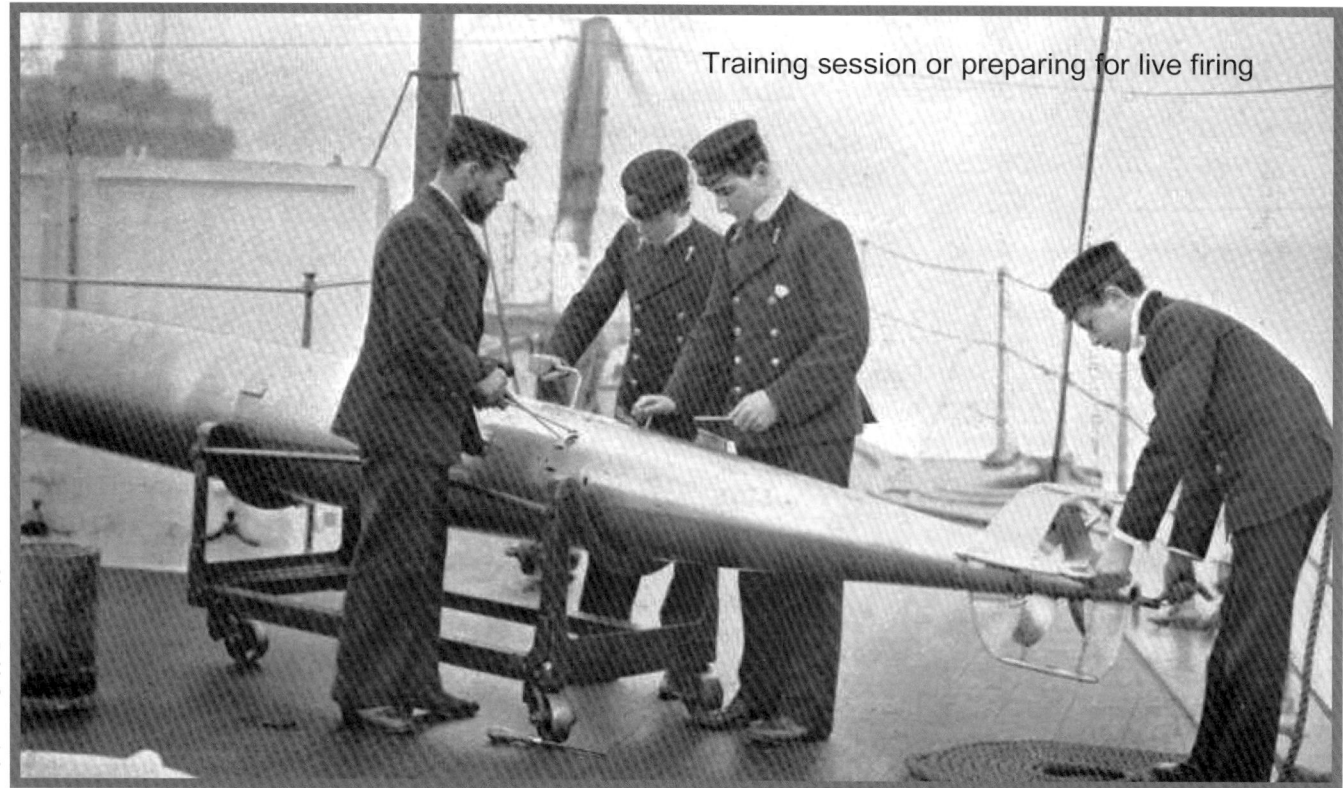

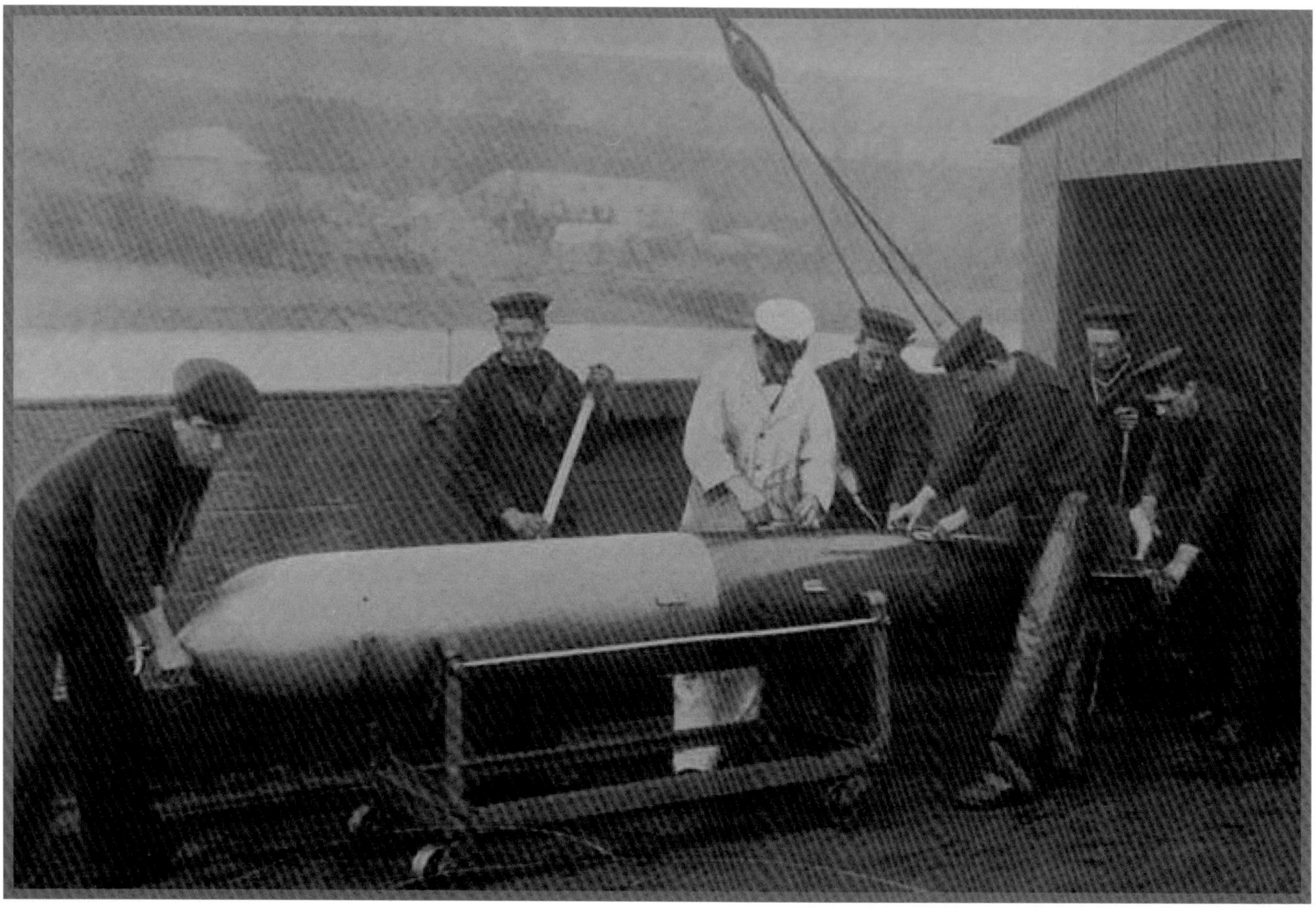

Courtesy Steve Johnson Cyberheritage

Fishing for a torpedo

To retrieve a practise torpedo a ring on the nose had to be 'caught' by a hook on the end of a line.

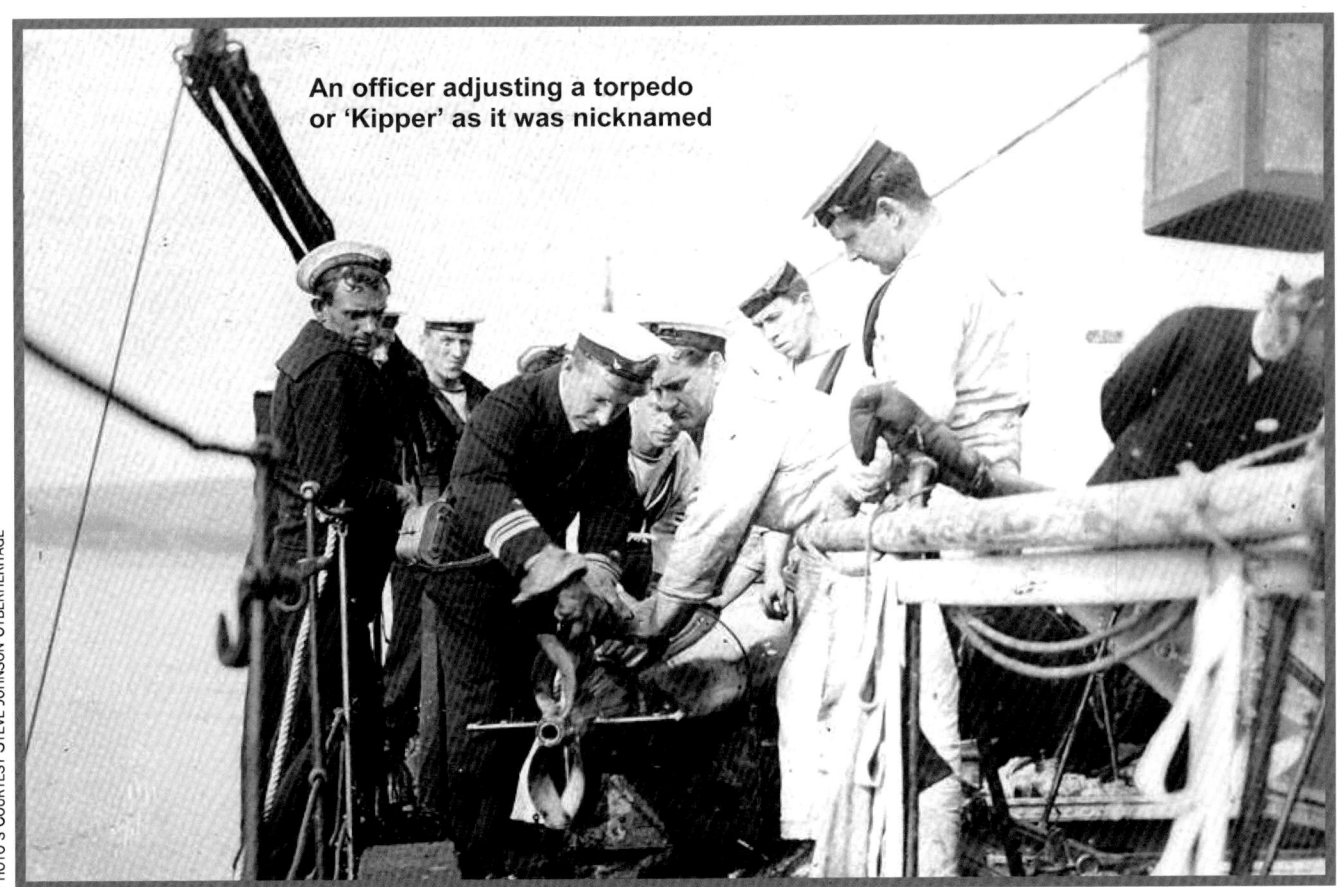

An officer adjusting a torpedo or 'Kipper' as it was nicknamed

OUTRIGGER TORPEDO

The photograph shows a steam pinnace on the River Lynher with an 18-inch 'Baby' torpedo suspended over the side by two pairs of tongs. When the two men release the rope at the same time the engine starts.

The torpedo is dropped into the water and will run in the direction that the boat is pointing. There is a steel shield before the funnel for the crew to muster in for shelter.

The charge is dropped 10 feet down and 32 feet from the bows of the boat; a gust of wind or turbulence and the torpedo would be way off target.

PHOTO W M CROCKETT PLYMOUTH

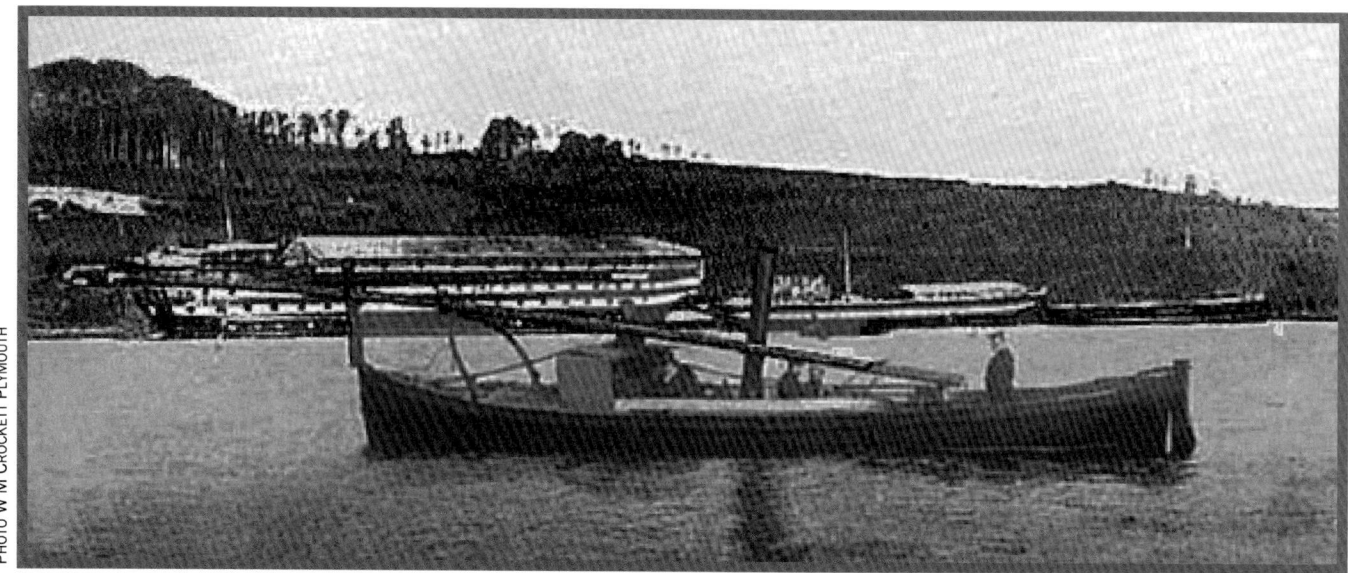

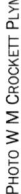

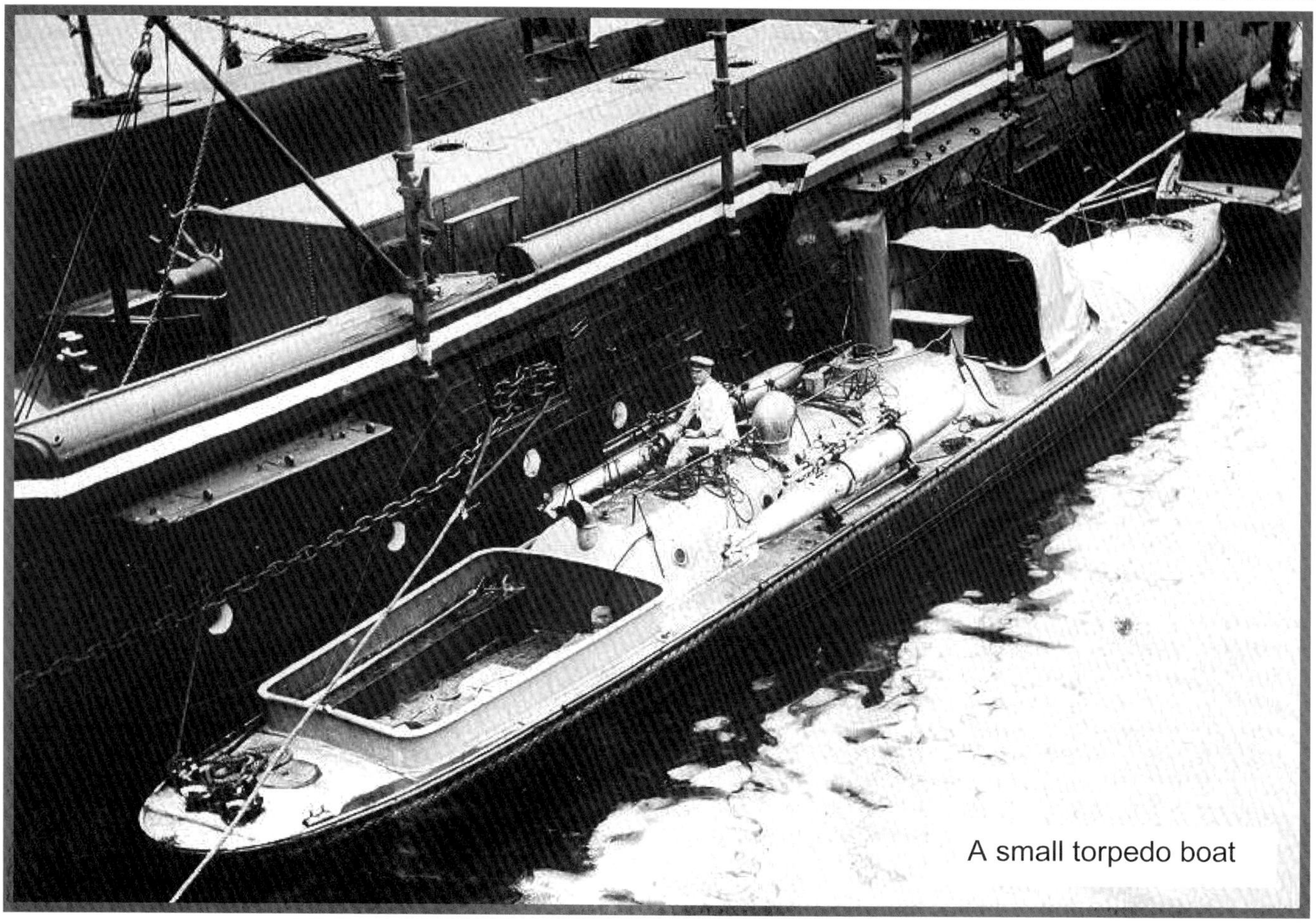

A small torpedo boat

PHOTO COURTESY STEVE JOHNSON CYBERHERITAGE

The torpedo explodes on impact with the rocks between Rame Head and Penlee Point - probably a small charge. This is an historic photograph of an incident that would not happen today. Now we can enjoy peaceful walks along the coast from the Coastguard Station, through Penlee Woods down into Cawsand.

Photo's Courtesy Steve Johnson Cyberheritage

Where is this one heading, toward the rocks at Penlee? Note the nose ring for retrieval.

This one is on its way to the target area

H.M.S. DEFIANCE WEARDE QUAY, SALTASH

As Colin Squires mentioned earlier on, the Defiance was never commissioned for service abroad but joined the ranks of the fine old ships that were laid up in the Hamoaze. Then, given a new role, she was moved into the Lynher estuary, in Cornwall, with the smaller hulks the Perseus and Flamingo ahead of her and connected by bridges.

The establishment at Wearde was a reproduction of the original Vernon school at Portsmouth, with the advantages of starting later, and thus being able to profit by the experience gained there. Every part of the internal economy and general routine of instruction was cut and dried to a nicety. The ship was beautifully clean, and the arrangements for the comfort and recreation of both officers and men were as perfect as possible. The lecture rooms were large and lofty, and the messes comfortable and roomy. When the school was in its infancy, and in the old frigate's cabins, which were utilised as lecture rooms, the space was confined and low, and very conducive to sleepiness in warm weather. In the bows were roomy lavatories and a gymnasium was close by.

On the main deck aft were the officer's messes and cabins, which extended along the deck for some distance also the galley and a very convenient room for drying the men's waterproofs. On the lower deck the Ship's Company lived, the Warrant Officers' mess being on the after part; below again there was on one side, a row of different patterns of above water discharging apparatus for the Whitehead torpedo, used for teaching the classes. Below this was a recreation room for the men that contained a billiard table, papers and magazines etc.

Next ahead of the Defiance was the 'Perseus', this vessel was used for mining work. There the mines were kept and fitted for use by the classes. Next ahead was the 'Flamingo' which was used principally for storing, testing and working electric cables; also fresh water was kept in tanks.
The beach and a portion of land (Wearde Quay) abreast the ship had been purchased by the Admiralty and utilised by the ship for various purposes. Amongst others there was an observing station, with range-finder for the minefield which was positioned a little way further up the creek. The position of the ship gave range for Whitehead torpedo exercises from her across the creek at all times of tide. This could not be done from the 'Vernon' at Portsmouth as all the runs with this torpedo having to be done from tenders with great loss of time.

The tenders to the Defiance were the 'Scourge' gunboat, two torpedo-boats and one destroyer. The 'Scourge' had an 18 inch tube for discharging torpedoes, made of aluminium, the only one in service at the time. All of the exercises from the vessels were carried out in Cawsand Bay, where outside of the breakwater was a Whitehead torpedo range. The instructing staff consisted, with the Captain, four Lieutenants, one Chief Torpedo Gunner, and several Warrant Officers, Torpedo Instructors, and Chief Torpedo Instructors.

The seamen in the Service who had volunteered for the rating of Seaman-Gunner would have been good character men. When rated they would have received extra pay, and held a special position, with regard to their training in the vessels they would have served such as the leading hand at the guns, special duties in the magazines and shell-rooms etc. And the mere fact of holding the rating gave a man a superior standing in the ship as a smart reliable seaman. Their pay would increase by 4 pence a day (old currency) for first class and 2 pence for second class certificates. The men could also increase their pay by becoming divers, instructors, adding 1 penny a day to their pay, with a further increase when actually diving. These seaman-gunners could then volunteer for the further rating of 'Seaman-Gunner Torpedo man' known as S.G.T. In one year the Defiance passed 782 men through the establishment.

The course of instruction for these men would last three months, divided into theoretical, practical, and Whitehead instructions. A Lieutenant and a certain number of instructors would take charge of each detachment of men, when they came, and would remain in charge of their instruction the whole time they were on board. Certain men who demonstrated superior ability were allowed to volunteer for the special ratings of 'Leading Torpedo Man' and 'Torpedo Instructor', adding 2 pence and 8 pence a day respectively to their pay, in addition to the 2 pence and 8 pence a day extra that the Seaman-Gunner got if he qualified as a 'Torpedo Man'. These men had a much longer and fuller course of instruction, and were, after a time, attached to some of the parties of men qualifying for S.G.T. to assist in the instruction, and gain more experience for the work they would have to do when rated. Thus a seaman who went in for the torpedo line would attain eventually to a pay of 4 shillings and 10 pence a day – that was if he attained the rank of 'Chief Torpedo Instructor' a trained diver, and re-engaged after his first term of twelve years completing his time for pension. If he passed for Warrant Officer, such as Boatswain or Gunner his pay and position was very superior and it was possible for him at the end of his career to retire with the rank of Lieutenant.

When the class attended a number of lectures they went entirely to practical work, fitting and laying out the various mines, etc. which had been taught in the lecture room. Everything was carried out as near as possible to the real thing only the mines were filled with dummy charges. During the annual manoeuvres in the summer the establishment was closed, all officers and men, with a few exceptions being sent in the mobilised ships and torpedo boats. At the termination of the exercise short leave was granted. Leave was also granted at Christmas.

The routine of life on board commenced at 9.00 a.m., by that time the ship had been cleaned, the liberty men brought off and all hands cleaned and breakfasted. The men fell in and inspected, prayers were read and then marched off to their various duties. There were three batches or 'Short Courses' going through the school at the same time, theory, practice and the other at Whitehead instructions. By 9.00 a.m. all classes had been prepared. At 11.50 a.m. the work was cleared up and the cooks departed to prepare for their messes and at noon it was "pipe to dinner". A 10 minute 'stand easy' was given during the forenoon, very acceptable to the men and instructors I would imagine. Instruction would commence at 1.00 p.m. and continued until 4.00 p.m. when the decks were cleared and the liberty men cleaned themselves for the shore. Later on those on board had supper and then after inspection retired for the evening. The same routine was continued until Friday when instruction ceased at 3.30 p.m. and the classes cleaned all the gear used during the week. On Saturdays there was no instruction, the forenoon being devoted to cleaning the ship and establishment and in the afternoon was 'Jack's' half-holiday.

Most of 'Jack's' life was spent on board ship and in foreign lands, or, waters, and during his service he had only flying visits to his home at long intervals. For this reason most of the married men would have had their wives and families near one of the home ports. In that way when in England they could see something of their families, so as much liberty as possible was given to the men, knowing that they would possibly be away for some years before seeing family and friends again. On board the Defiance there was a regular staff of pensioners and others for keeping the ship clean.

To keep men on board trying to qualify was kept to a minimum, a few to man the pumps etc. in case of fire and the watches to be maintained.

Returning to the instruction having passed their classroom course work and lectures the men would commence drill at the discharging tubes and do a considerable amount of shooting with them from the Defiance and from torpedo boats attached to her. Classes were taken out to Cawsand Bay, their dinners sent out to them. When the course was completed they were examined and rated. The largest course of all was for 'Torpedo Instructor' which took eight months.

The whole establishment was supplied with electricity for lighting etc. Plenty of skills were found amongst the artificers; they would maintain and repair the electrical instruments. Captain Jackson had already made very interesting discoveries with wireless communications. The Whitehead torpedo had been developed into a most reliable weapon, and had been continually improved with experimental work carried out in the torpedo schools, an equal amount of attention had been given to improving the methods of discharging. The submerged tubes ejecting the torpedo from the ship's bottom some distance below the water line being the preferred method. The officers of the staff were chosen from the torpedo Lieutenant's list, the Captain, usually having been a Torpedo Officer originally.

HMS Defiance with the 'Vernon' at Portsmouth was for the purpose of specially training a percentage of seamen in the use of the mines and torpedoes carried by the Royal Navy, not to be exclusively used by them, but that they would have been a crew of experienced men to take the principal duties to instruct and lead others.

Also for the instruction of all executive officers whether on full or half pay, so as to keep themselves posted up in the latest ideas. This included retired officers who had volunteered to serve at sea in the case of war breaking out and wished to keep themselves up with the times in torpedo work.

A practise exercise in the river Lynher

PHOTO W M CROCKETT PLYMOUTH

J111136 Roberts W. Chief Petty Officer with his wife Violet May

Phyllis Crawford, who lives in Forder, Saltash, has shared with me some wonderful memories of her late Father, William John Roberts. He joined the navy as a boy in 1924 and started his training at HMS Impregnable. He eventually joined HMS Defiance Wearde Quay 17th July 1929, after serving on various ships including HMS Revenge and HMS Hood. In October 1929, he qualified as a Seaman Torpedo Man and in July 1934, a Leading Torpedo Man and eventually on the 4th July 1943, a Torpedo Gunners Mate. He was also skilled in heavy current engineering that included all D.C. equipment from dynamos and generators, lighting and wiring, also light current engineering, instruments, practical use of tools and lifting appliances, tackles etc...

Other naval ships and 'stone frigates' that William served on included HMS Vivid (to become HMS Drake), HMS Dorsetshire, Cheshire, Lochinvar and Renown. He also served on the Queen Elizabeth from the 7th May 1930 to the 6th February 1933. In civilian life on leaving school aged 14 he was employed as an errand boy. William retired from the navy aged forty as a Chief Petty Officer after 24 years of exemplary service. The remarks recorded by his Torpedo Officer on HMS Defiance, Wilcove, on his certificate states: *'A most trustworthy and conscientious Chief Electrician. He is keen and smart, with a good power of command. A man who will prove an excellent asset to any employer.'* The assessment was endorsed by the Captain of HMS Drake. William had experienced more in his 24 years of naval life (inc war at sea and on land) than most others in their lifetime.

Two similar photographs but worthy of a mention. The top photograph was loaned by Kay Wilson of 'Diving Belle' a business that operates from Wearde Quay. It gives another angle of Wearde Quay with the railway embankment that can be seen between the trees to the right of the picture.

Below: The landing jetty at the shore side of the Defiance, to the right of the steps is a large dummy sea mine on the quayside. It appears to be an open day for visitors. Perhaps tea with the Captain? You can see the crew rowing visitors out to the ship. It must have been an important day for HMS Defiance, note the civilians dressed in their Sunday best.

Upwards and towards the 'Defiance Halt' platform, 80 plus sailors on shore leave with a few 'bob' in their pockets to spend. Above the quay can be seen the cultivated fields where the residents grew and supplied a considerable amount of fresh vegetables to the Defiance. Today on the embankment there are allotments. The effect of the re-location of the HMS Defiance establishment to Wilcove must have had a profound effect on the local economy. To the right of the picture can be seen the boathouse with a large building behind.

Pictured below: (left) All that remains of that same building.

Below: (right) Author's wife Sue stood on the steps leading up to the 'Halt' as they are today.

THE DEFIANCE HALT AND PLATFORM

'Defiance Halte' (it was formerly spelt with an e) platform situated between Saltash and St. Germans. The first reference appears to have been on the 22nd February 1905 with the GWR seeking permission from the Board of Trade to 'construct and bring into use this stopping place.' The Halt opened on the 1st March 1905 and was inspected on the 7th June by Colonel Yorke, who recommended that the platform be reached by two pathways, one for the public and the other leading to the Admiralty landing place. Before long the GWR wrote to the Board of Trade, on the 14th July 1905, with a proposal to build a 'new Defiance Halt' on the deviation line, between Saltash and St.Germans with improved facilities. This time a 259ft platform was proposed on each side of the up and down lines, with alcoves at the west end of each platform and steps to the road over bridge, this was opened on an unknown date again by Colonel Yorke who stated: *"I have inspected the Halte for rail motor cars which has been constructed between Saltash and St. Germans on the GWR. The Halte consists of two platforms each 350ft long and 7ft wide and 3ft above the rail level. Each platform has a small shelter as well as lamps and name boards. The Halte is on the new deviation lines between mile 151½ and 152¼. The arrangements being satisfactory, I can recommend its utilisation."*

Defiance Halt was renamed Defiance Platform from the 1st May 1906 with parcel traffic being handled. Shortly after opening the platform was extended to 400ft and eventually toilets were added. Listed in the GWR 'Traffic Dealt with at Stations' statistics, it is shown as having a staff of four in 1913, 1923 and in 1929 and with a staff of two in 1930.

Early photographs show the platform constructed of timber, but in photographs taken after the closure, the platforms are built of brick and paving, date of rebuilding unknown.

The station officially closed in October 1930, the up platform and building remained in a good state of repair and was used in the spring and summer for loading flowers and some garden produce onto up trains until 1957.

Sailors walking up the lane from Defiance to the station, there was a short cut before the bridge that led down to the Halt.

Shore leave for some of the Ship's Company; the train operated a suburban service into Plymouth and Millbay Station adjacent to Union Street in Plymouth, with its array of public houses this would have been an attraction, also, a visit to Home Park to support Plymouth Argyle or perhaps to support the visiting team from their home town on a Saturday afternoon. The photograph circa 1908 shows a motor train and they were powered by steam engines situated in the chassis of the coaches. The Halt eventually had waiting rooms, toilets and Station Master's ticket office.

Top: Pictured today, the steps leading to the platform at 'Defiance Halt' the remains of which can still be seen. Below: The Author's wife Sue with daughter Kaye and grandchildren Florence and Rose at the gateway to the 'down-line'.

Unfortunately, the two iron 'kissing' gates are gradually rusting and falling apart. One was used for the 'up' platform and one for the 'down' platform. How nice it would be to see the gates restored with a plaque commemorating the history of that important and strategic site.

Steve Johnson further up the River Lynher is beside an Admiralty boundary stone, complete with an anchor cut into it. The old mine adit might have been used as a range finding and observation post during live firing.

Tony Marsh, Saltash

I was born at Wearde Quay in 1950, in the end terraced house that faces you as you walk down Wearde hill. I can't remember the address, the Pollards and Reg Cockburn also lived in the terrace.

We used Defiance Halt Station (which was overgrown and deserted) to catch the train to Plymouth and return. More often than not only a few passengers would be on the train after departing from Saltash Station. The short cut to the station for us was to walk under the twin tunnels just up the road from the end cottage.

To visit Fore Street from Wearde Quay we walked the Antony Estate

footpath at the rear of the cottage, through the fields, pass the sewage works, up a footpath and over Coombe Creek via the footbridge attached to the railway viaduct. (See photograph with attached footpath).

The pathway led back down to Coombe Road via a gate at the top of Coombe Road hill, just before the road goes under the railway line.

8 COOMBE AND ALBERT BRIDGES, SALTASH

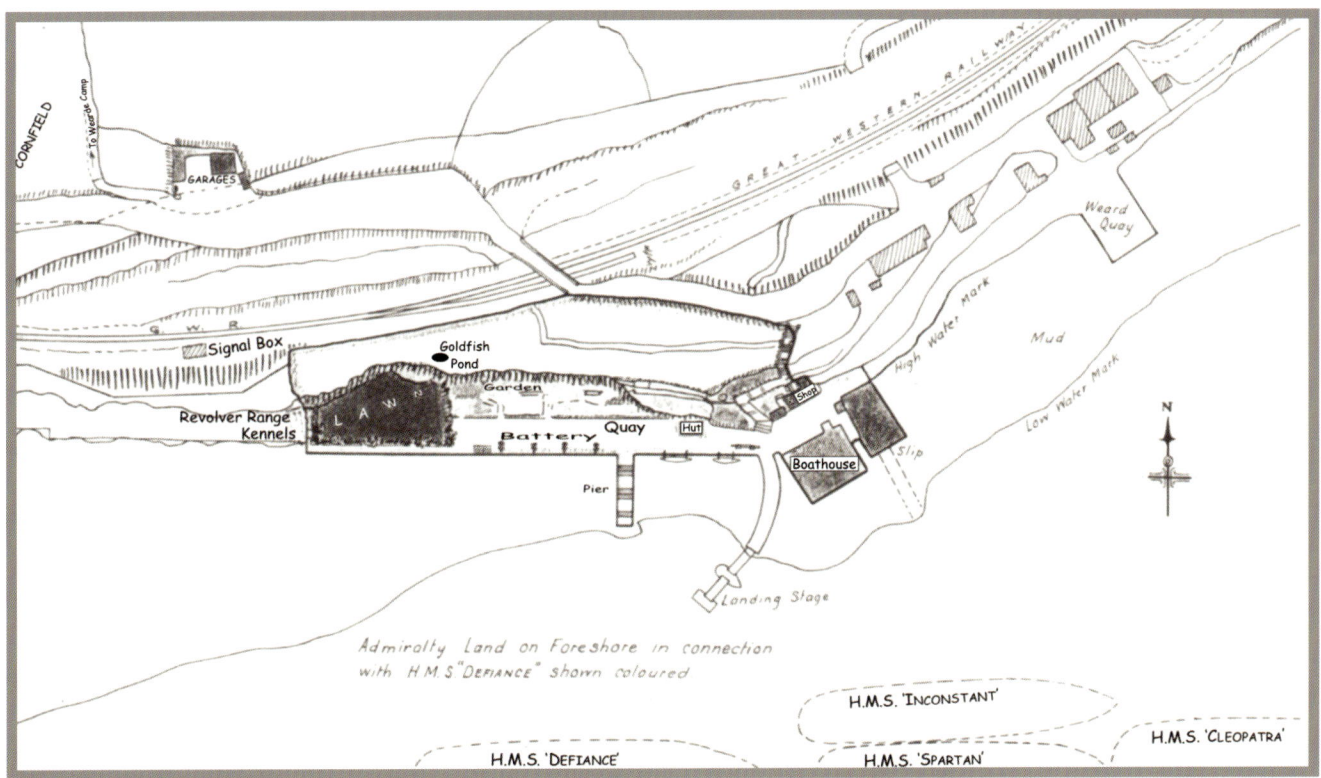

Above: Map drawn by Lt. Cdr.Ouvry August 1927 for the Admiralty. The shop on the quay was run by the Pearce Family, who served the Defiance for many years and also when the establishment relocated to Wilcove.
Below: The shore side of Defiance in recent times after the closure of the establishment. It is difficult to imagine the industry with the hustle and bustle of everyday life that pervaded there.

Thank you to Grierson and 'Rolima' and boat trip for photo.   Diving Belle moored.

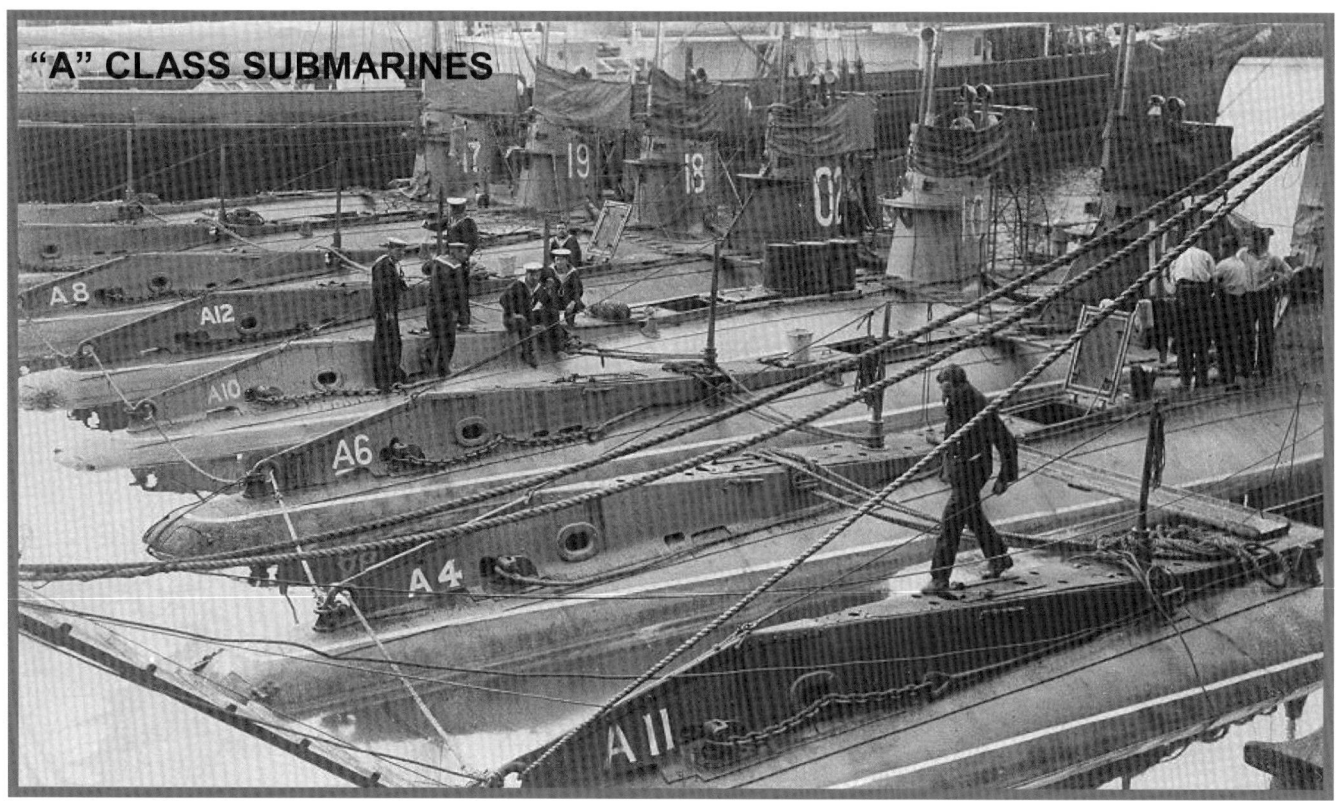

"A" CLASS SUBMARINES

Thursday 8th June 1905 was a fateful day for the Royal Navy at Plymouth, and especially so for the fated crew of Submarine A8. Leaving Plymouth for exercises off Looe in tandem with her sister boat the A7. After reaching Plymouth Breakwater, an initial dive ended in the A8 surfacing. The crew of an escorting surface Torpedo boat spotted that the A8 was in trouble. The A8 had developed a list and was sitting lower and lower in the water until she slid below the water bow first, showing her stern to the sky. She vanished and the lives of 14 brave men and one officer were lost, some lucky ones including the Commanding Officer, Lt A.H.C.Candy got clear, primarily because they were standing on the submarine casing. Tons of water came through a faulty hatch seal, filling the boat so it became negatively buoyant and all trim was lost.....the end was inevitable and as she sank, sea water at a higher pressure that the air in the boat would have slammed the hatch shut. These early boats were petrol fuelled and the account follows that there was shortly afterwards what appeared to be an underwater explosion.

On Monday 12th June the A8 was raised and transported to Devonport Dockyard where the dead were removed with great dignity and respect. The funeral was on Thursday 15th June. Most of the deceased are buried close to each other in the Ford Park Cemetery.

The whole populace of the Three Towns as it was then, Plymouth, Devonport and Stonehouse, all turned out to pay their final respects to what had become a local disaster. Streets were thronged with masses as the funeral procession wound its way from the Dockyard Chapel to Ford Park Cemetery, the half mile long procession took 90 minutes to cover 2 miles......eleven were buried in the cemetery and four in their home towns. The flag draped coffins were carried on gun carriages pulled by sailors, anchors made of flowers, sailors marched with rifles, a military band played. The whole of the Three Towns stopped. At the graveside a military funeral with full honours paid respect to those who locals called *'Heroes all of Them'*.

The A8 herself was recommissioned, but being able to only stay at sea for a day, having to return to a Depot ship at night, and only armed with two torpedoes, her usefulness was limited with the fast advances of this new infant naval technology. Each day she would have one of her two crews on board, alternating. No man having to spend more than one full day aboard. Launched at Barrow on 23rd January 1905, and for the reasons above having not been much involved in World War I, she was scrapped in 1920 by Philip & Son of Dartmouth, Devon.

Sadly over the years the graves of the A8 had been neglected and vandalised, but having been taken over by the Ford Park Cemetery (Charitable) Trust in the year 2000 and managed on behalf of the people of Plymouth. The hard working Trust has raised the necessary funding to tidy the graves and all the headstones have been restored; the Trust is to be congratulated and also the assistance rendered by the young sailors from the Submarine School of HMS Raleigh. The graves were rededicated on the 15th June 2005 with the Cadets in attendance and a Piper playing "The Flowers of the Forest"; followers found it both haunting and moving.

It is interesting to note that HMS A1 and A5 had already been lost on trials and in total six of the 13 A-boats launched before 1914 had foundered or sunk before the war, some naval personnel began to give the name *'instruments of collective suicide'*.

The A1 was struck by the liner Berwick Castle in 1904 and sank with all hands. The A3 collided with her own depot ship and sank immediately. A4 was sunk at Devonport in 1905 when the wash of a passing ship flooded her ventilators, and the A5 was badly damaged by two petrol explosions also in 1905. The A7 was sunk with all hands in Whitsand Bay in 1914, and the A9 foundered just outside Plymouth in 1906 after being hit by the steam ship Coath. Luckily she managed to resurface and no one was hurt, but two years later petrol fumes killed four of her crew. These unsettling disasters had the effect of virtually halting the flow of submarine volunteers leading in some cases, to men refusing to sail on what they thought were unsafe boats.

< *Looking at the eight submarines lined up together and the faint image of the shore in all probability they were in the River Lynher, moored for the night with the A7 and A9. Pennant numbers 17 and 19 in the lower facing page photograph.*

Stephen Birch with his Brother in Law Joseph Spencer

Great Uncle Stephen Birch age 23 was a submarine pioneer training in the Holland Submarine Boat No. 4 at a time when the service was less than 300 strong. He died in the explosion in the A8 when on her second trip out on the 8th of June 1905 with a double crew (nineteen on board with the four survivors being on deck at the time,) for training, she blew up 400 yards outside of the western end of the Plymouth Breakwater killing fifteen men.

Explosions in submarines were not uncommon, until the A13 class when the diesel engine replaced the petrol engine; petrol and electric motors were a fatal combination in an enclosed space.

The funeral on the 15th of June 1905 was the biggest seen in Plymouth for many years and King Alfonso of Spain at the time visiting England sent his condolences. There were over twenty thousand residents of the 'Three Towns, Plymouth, Devonport and Stonehouse,' lining the route to Ford Park Cemetery with my Grandmother Mary Roche (nee Birch) in the procession behind her Brother's coffin, which was pulled by thirty sailors. Newspaper reports stated that many women with babes in their arms were in the crowds that lined the route, *'that lives with me always, the very symbol of a Naval Town such as Plymouth.'*

Courtesy of Chris Roche, great nephew of Stephen Birch, Submariner A8.

FUNERAL OF THE CREW OF AN 'A CLASS' SUBMARINE

The three photographs show the funeral cortège from Devonport to Ford Park Cemetery.
Top left: Visible is the old Devonport Railway Station, Kings Road, where the college now stands. Top right: Officers in full dress uniform.
Below: The coffins traditionally drawn on a gun carriage by fellow shipmates.

REVERSE SIDE OF THE CARD FEATURED ON THE FRONT COVER

Posted in Devonport 17th February 1913
with a 10.30 p.m. date stamp.

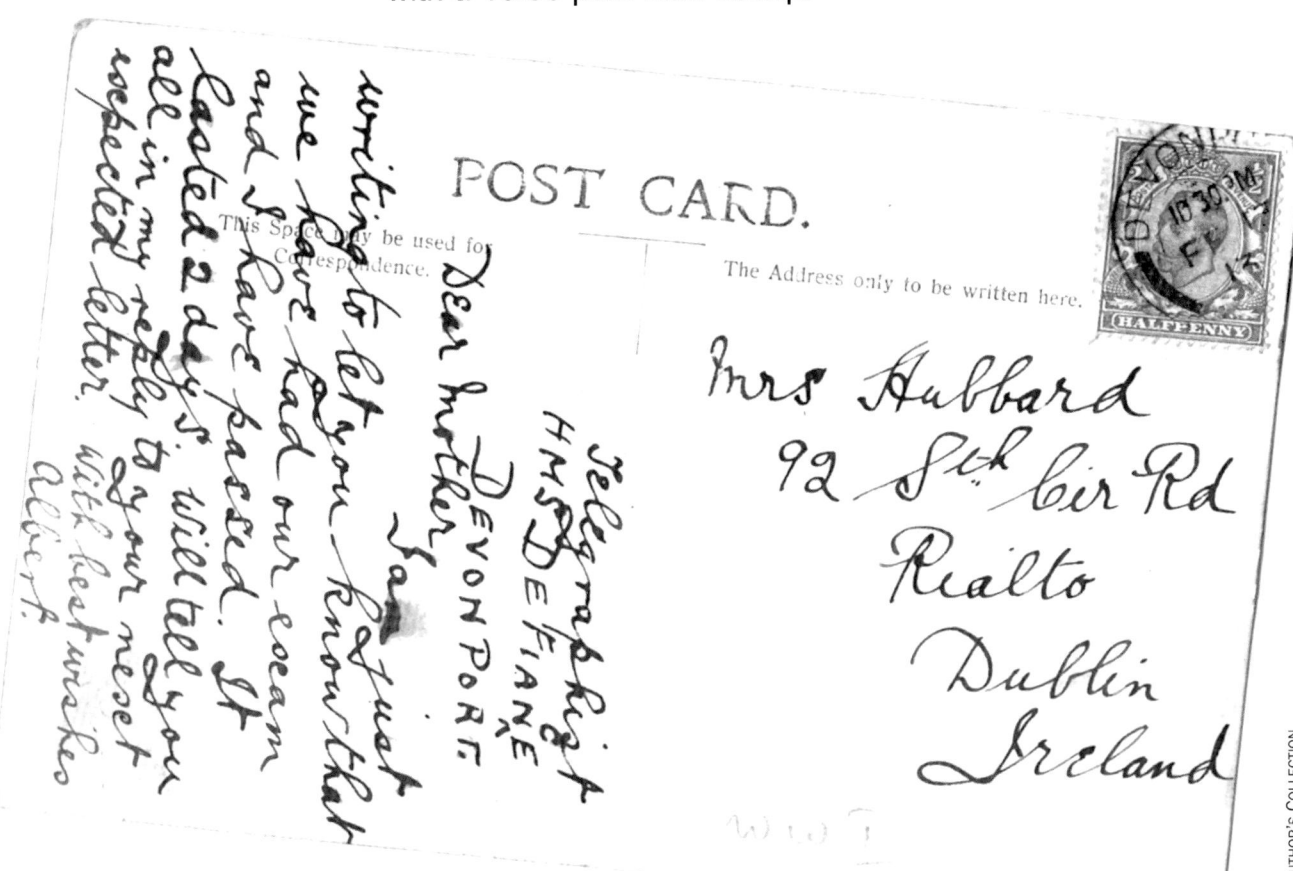

To: Mrs Hubbard
      92 Sth Cir Rd
      Rialto
      Dublin
      Ireland

From: Telegraphist
      HMS Defiance

Dear Mother,
I am just writing to let you know that we have had our exam and I have passed. It lasted 2 days. Will tell you all in reply to your next expected letter.

With best wishes,
Albert

HMS Defiance Wilcove Devonport

How many lads are there who spent time on this ship before getting a draft to somewhere or something only to come back to 35 Mess and go out again? Just about every ship or mother ship had an EA of some rating and we were supposed to finish training knowing the layout of supplies to all of them. Town class, County class, frigates, carriers, battleships, the lot. The class room was hot and stuffy in summer or freezing in winter and those sketches kept on coming down and going up again at a rapid rate.

Just for strangers to that excellent ship it comprised three old tubs lashed together with gangways between - HMS Andromeda which originally had sails as well as engines, she was a prize from the French sometime in the 1800 hundreds - HMS Inconstant, steel hulled - HMS Vulcan with a wooden bottom which used to be copper sheathed until it was discovered with salt water they had a battery between the two ships, so they took the copper off. All three were hardly sea going because, being anchored for years, they had become settled in mud. This meant you didn't get rocked to sleep.

Theory instruction was dispensed by Officers, practical work by Chiefs. We learnt maths, electrical principles, RN history (official and unofficial), how torpedoes worked, trimming gyros, sound powered telephones, Y-dischargers, depth charges, machine shop practise, fitting skills and other bits and pieces. The best bit of fun was fire fighting and use of breathing apparatus in smoke filled ships. There was one fire alarm on Androm which I had to attend fully kitted. There was a small fire which I found and extinguished, I never admitted I had started it accidentally.

Torpedoes were very interesting; a 21" torpedo had a four cylinder engine and using diesel fuel compressed by 3,000 lb air which caused ignition. The housing was 21" diameter and perhaps 12" long. It had to be stripped and rebuilt for practise. Just about everyone finished assembly with a pipe of some sort left in their box that could not be put in, - so strip and try again. A gyro driven by the 3,000 lb air provided guidance. They had to be trimmed so that on start up the top pivot did not describe a spiral. This required adjusting tiny little screws and could take ages.

The workshop equipment looked old enough to have come from the 1800's. The Nile centre lathe with speed control using two pairs of adjustable cones and a vee belt. As one pair opened the other pair closed giving infinitely variable speed. The chiefs' weren't quite as old as the lathe but on joining the ship I swopped my hard glazed collars for his soft ones, we were both delighted. Working in a white shirt and black tie took some getting used to, especially as I didn't mind getting dirty.

Each mess had messmen who drew our food from the galley and dished it out to us. Who can forget the Saturday dinner? Every one who could was going ashore, including the messmen, so dinner was quick to prepare and quick to clear up. The menu for the day was, - Mashed potatoes (cool), boiled beetroot (cold) and herring in tomato (cold). A sixpenny "tater oggy" at the station was much preferred.

We also had a mess president who supplemented the food and dealt with our rum ration, neat for petty officers and above, watered down rum (grog) for leading hands and below. Rum was drawn from the spirit store under a guard of marines, taken up to the quarter deck of Inconstant and measured out one tot per rating. Any left over, there was never too little, was tipped into the scuppers in full view of all. Although illegal according to Admiralty instructions, it was a currency you could buy favours with or use as a birthday present. You were also not supposed to take it ashore or to save it for future use. Schemes for collecting the tipped away rum were not unknown.

There were two routes for going ashore. Route one, row across to Wilcove landing stage and walk a couple of miles down into Torpoint to get the chain ferry across to Devonport. You relied on the ships boat crew to row you across unless you had influence. Route two; take the ferry, quite frequently the Totnes Castle (a paddle steamer with a fixed shaft between paddles, had a 1/4 mile turning circle) that took you to the Flagstaff steps in Devonport Dockyard, the gate of which was guarded. This could cause problems for adventurous smugglers of rum or tobacco. Was your name written on the toilet walls of the Torpoint Church tea bar? If so did you have to pay towards re-painting? Mine wasn't on the wall! If anyone can add to this story please do so.

Petty Officer L. Mason EA 4th Class DMX645610
WW2 Peoples War BBC

MY LARGE FLAT FOOT

Sailors often went barefooted on board. It is impossible to say when the habit ceased; in general terms, in such ships as destroyers from the mid-1890s, with iron decks and iron ladders, shoes would have normally been worn. As late as the 1930s, some of the ship's crew might have gone barefoot. The practice died out in the First World War.

Life was hard on board a navy vessel but the following few pages gives us an insight into the off duty and lighter side of life.

THE LEADING HAND'S STORY

A little 'yarn' or 'thread' from Albert Richardson RN. MBE. A very knowledgeable character with so many stories about the navy and the rivers around Saltash.

Albert rowed across the river from Antony Passage to Jupiter Point for many years. He was The Leading Hand of Boat Repairers for HMS Raleigh.

Ritchie's story,

Mrs. Joyce Arrowsmith, one time Landlady of The Cecil Arms, St. Stephens discovered a barrel of beer missing from her establishment. The evening before, a group of sailors from Defiance had frequented the 'pub' and on departing from the premises could not resist the lifting or rolling of a barrel of beer.

The local constabulary were informed and found to their concealed amusement the tracks of the sailors and the barrel, leading up over the field and down to HMS Defiance, because that evening and night there had been a very heavy frost, so 'Jack was caught because of the Frost'.

The men were apprehended and ordered to parade in front of the Captain's table as defaulters and to suffer the consequences.

H.M.S. Defiance (near Saltash)

Quoits— a throwing game using a coil of rope.

Rolling the grass pitch up at the sports field. Football or cricket?

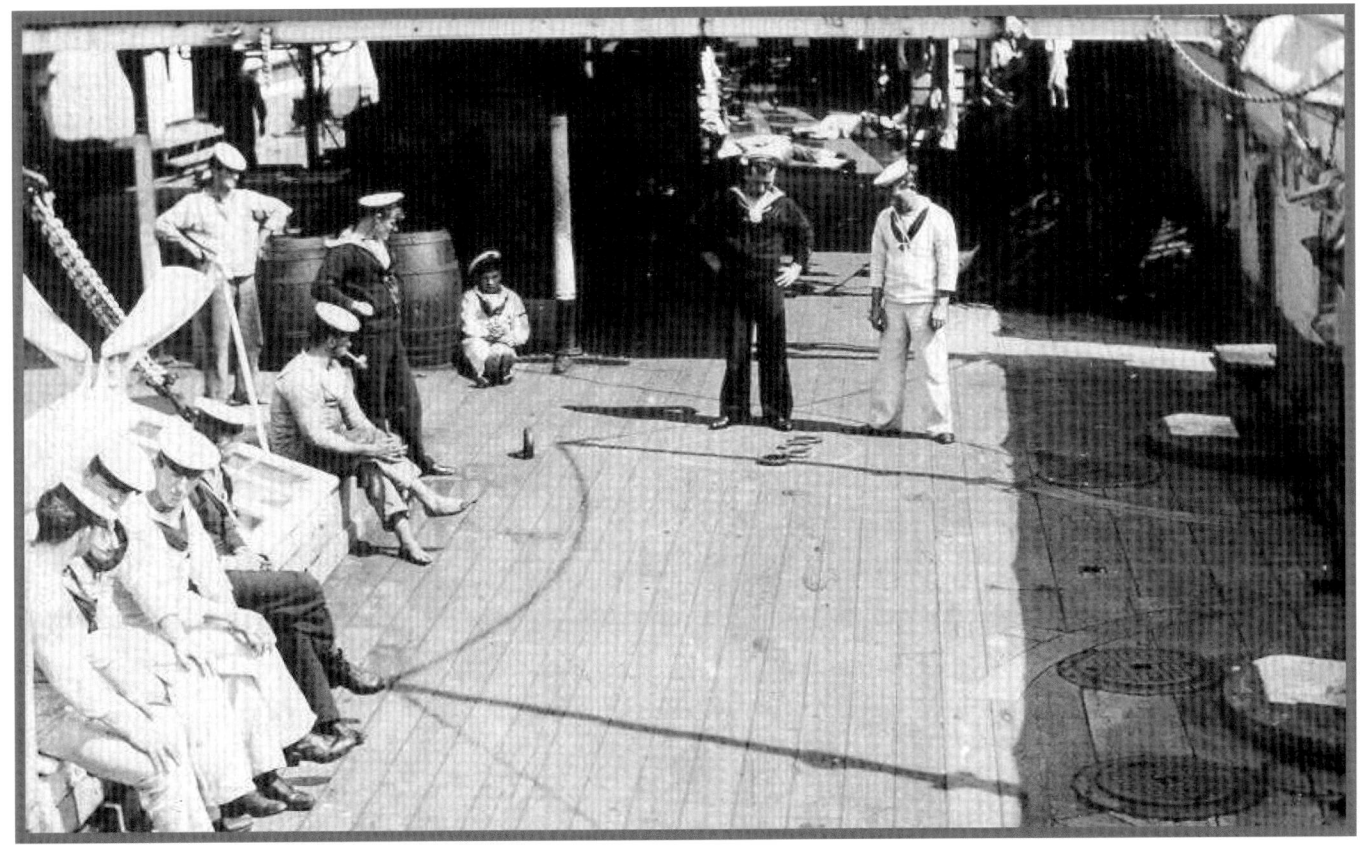

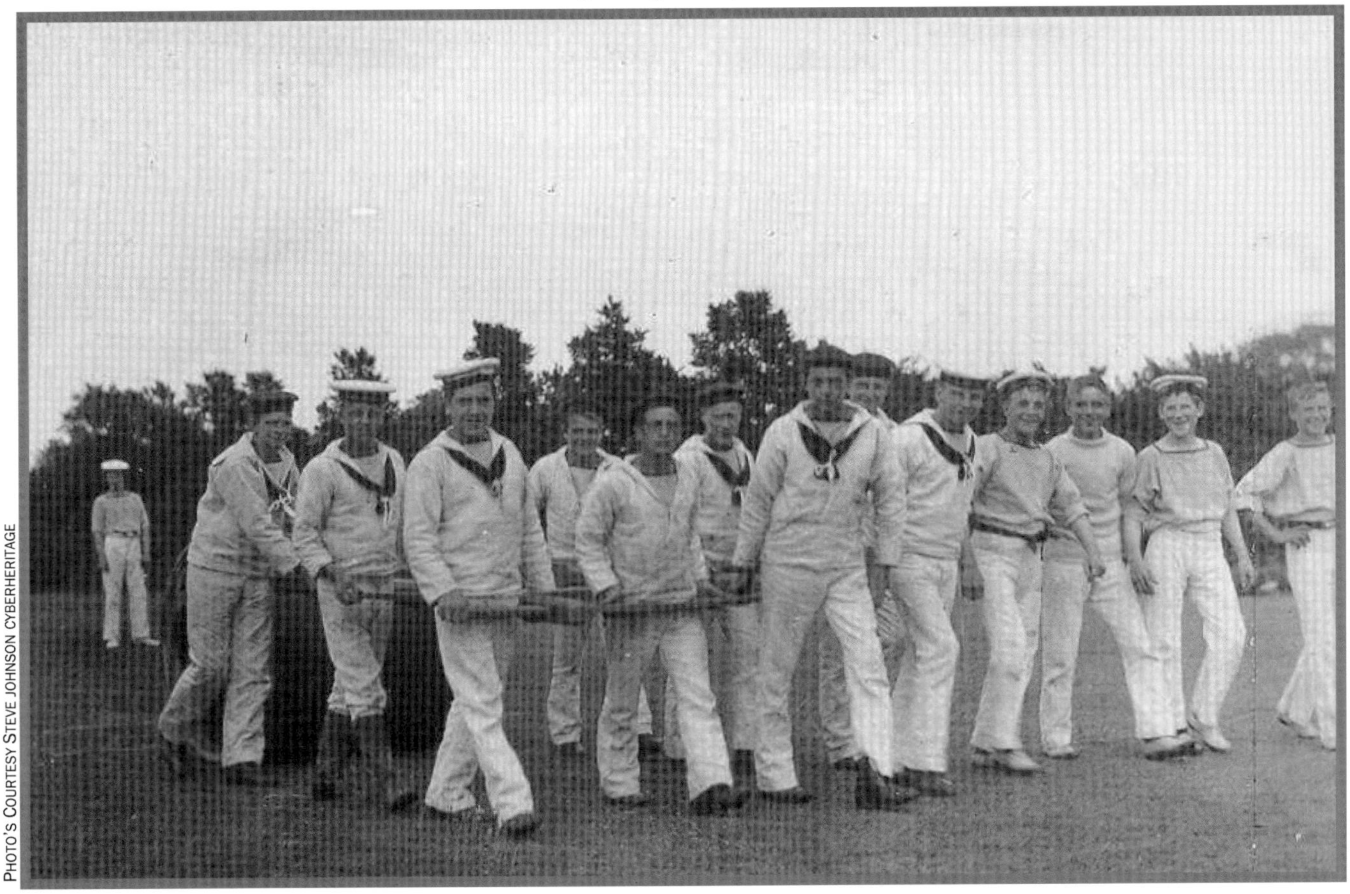

PHOTO'S COURTESY STEVE JOHNSON CYBERHERITAGE

The crew of Defiance, one of the ship's photographers sitting in the front row third from the left with his hands clasped.

Sailors from HMS Defiance relaxing, they certainly enjoyed their clay pipes, pieces of which are still being found in the gardens and on the foreshore by the residents of Wearde Quay.

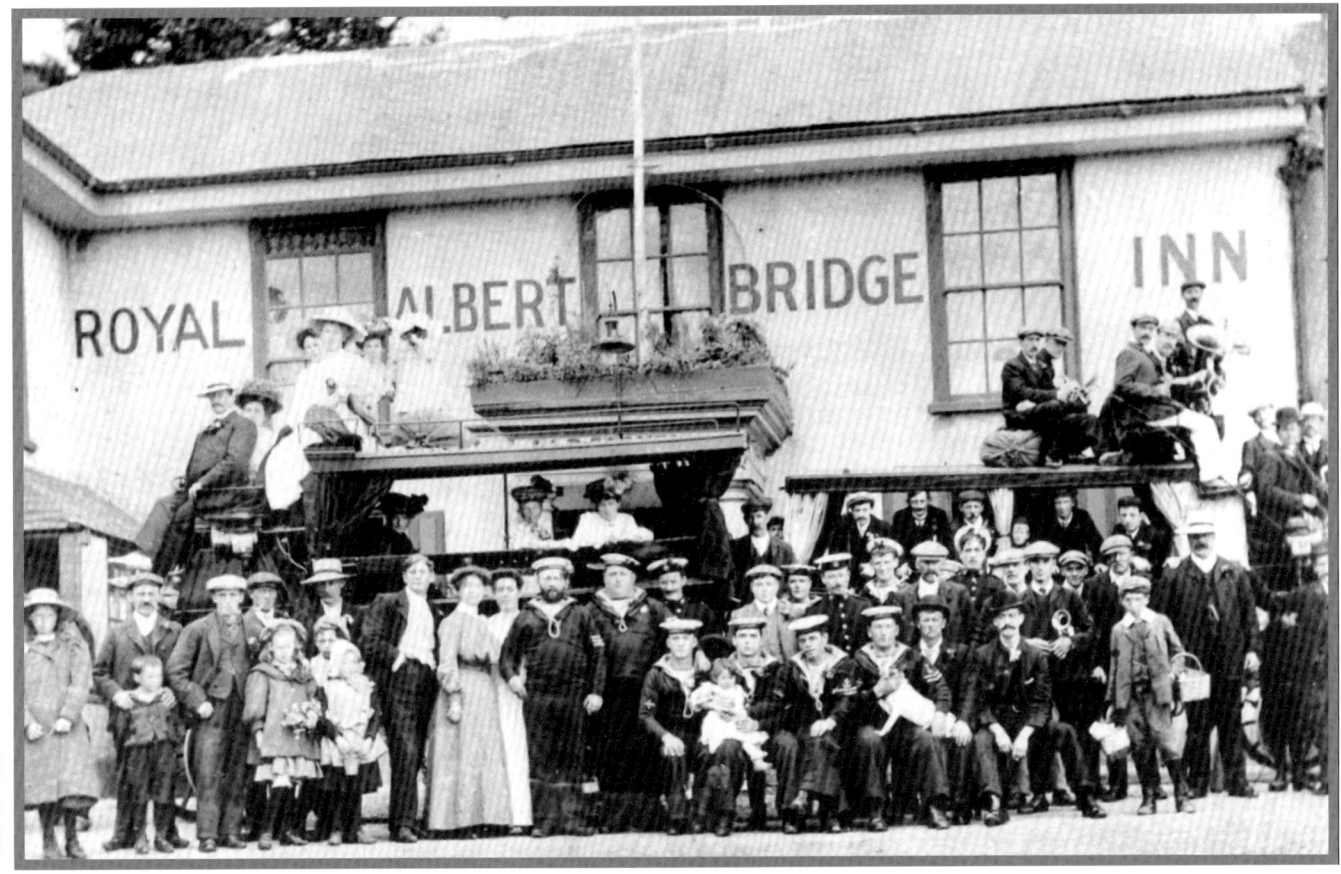

A picture of an outing to the *Royal Albert Bridge Inn at Saltash Passage.*
There could be sailors in the picture from HMS Defiance who settled into the area and raised families. The Author's Great Grandfather originally from Manchester who was in the Navy in the 1880's also settled and raised a family in the area, and frequented the Inn. My Grandparents lived just above in Vicarage Gardens. I remember watching the steam trains pass the rear garden and sometimes stop to take water from the tank situated there, just before the little road bridge.
The Royal Albert Bridge Inn was originally called the Dock Inn but the name was changed when the bridge was built. This annual wagonette outing in 1908 drew friends from the Wheatsheaf at Saltash and many serving naval ratings.

Below: A gathering of the crew of HMS Defiance.

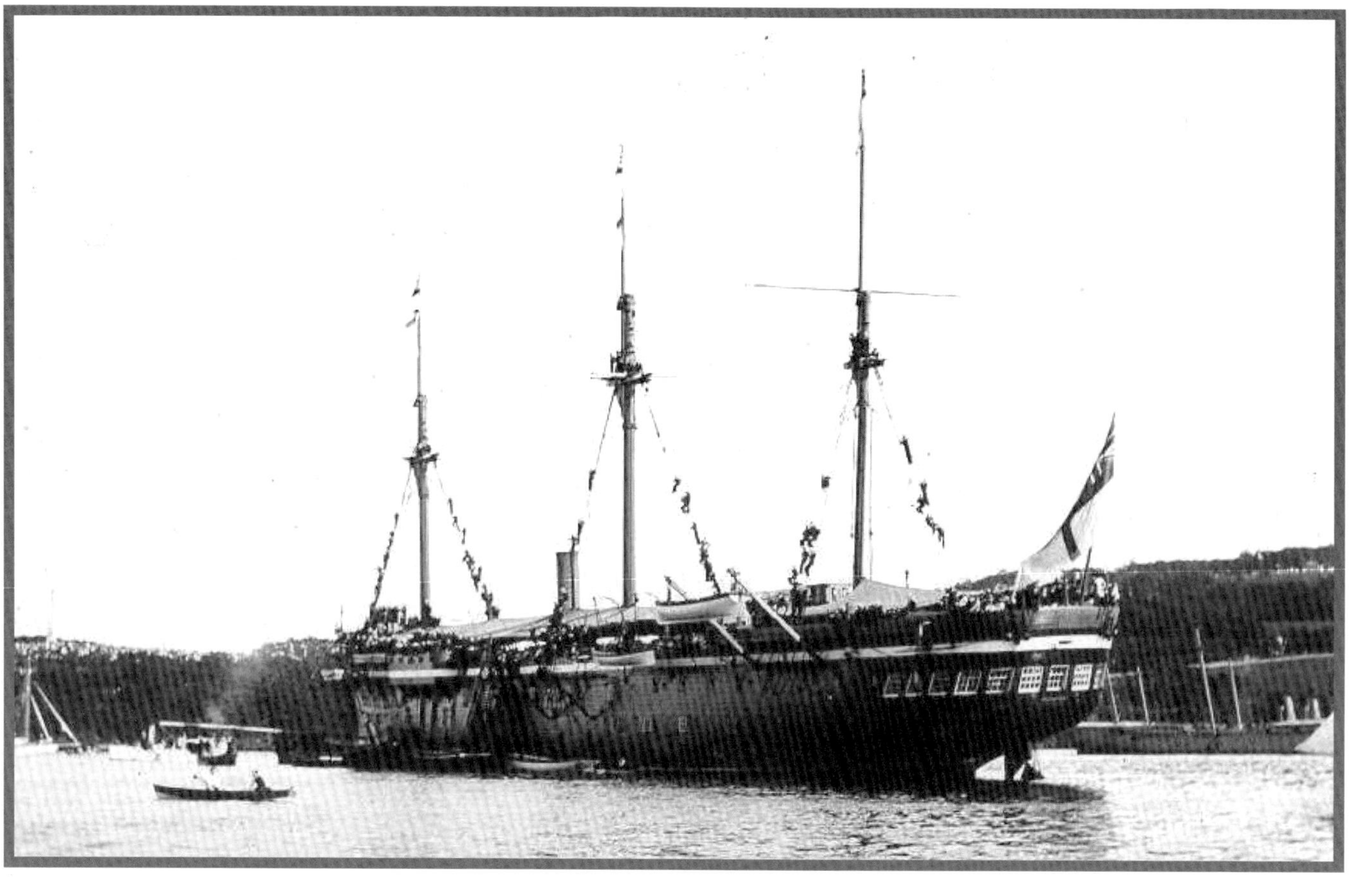

Above: Sailors aloft in this shot of a 'Hulk' moored nearby 'Defiance'.

Below: 'The Captain's comfortable cabin'.

PHOTO'S COURTESY STEVE JOHNSON CYBERHERITAGE

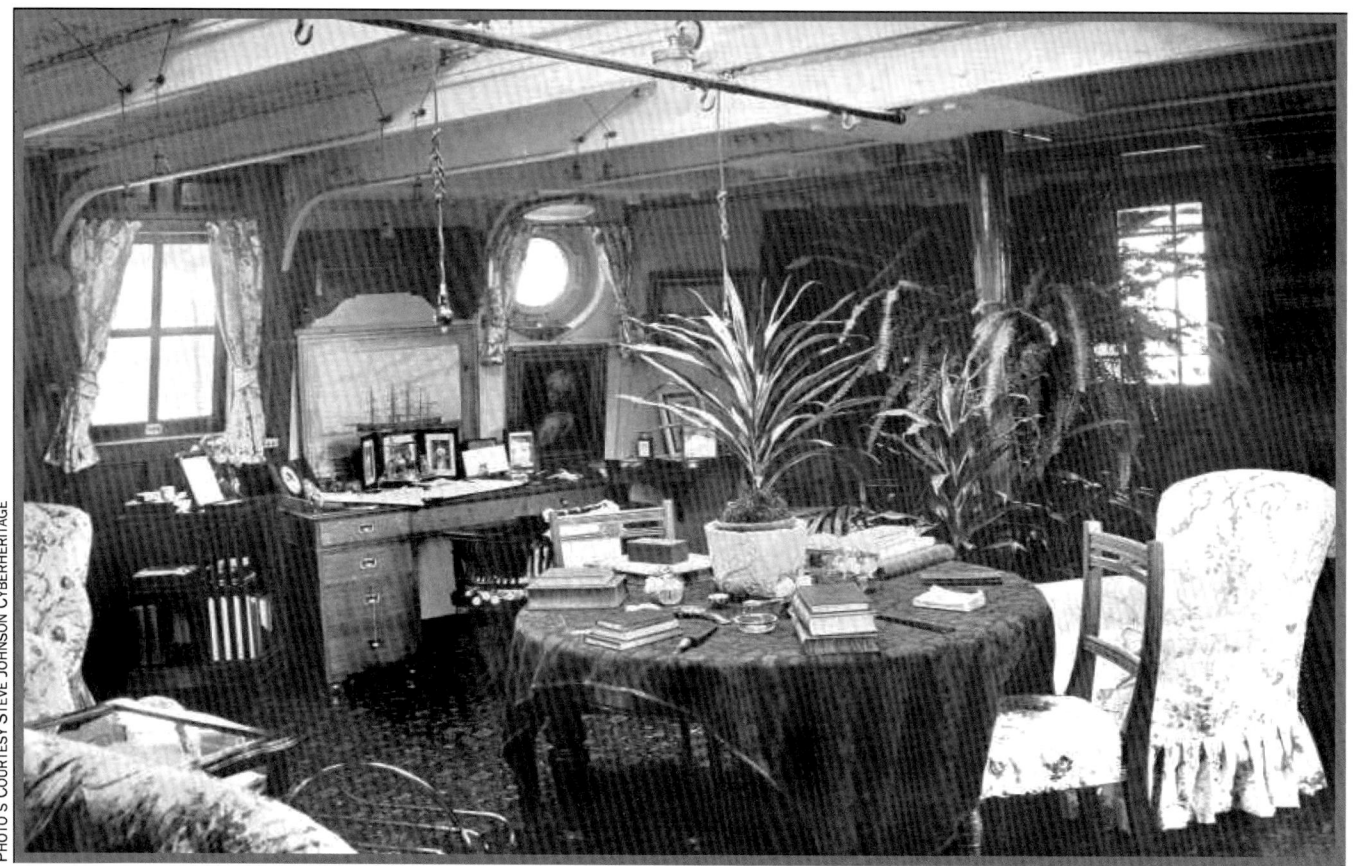

TWELVE ROYAL NAVY SHIPS HAVE BEEN NAMED DEFIANCE

- The first Defiance was a pinnace of 8 guns that took part in the action against the Spanish Armada in 1588.

- The second Defiance was a 46-gun galleon built in 1590 and sold in 1650.

- The third Defiance was a 10-gun ship that served with the Royalists during the English Civil War. She foundered in 1652 in the West Indies.

- The fourth Defiance was a 66-gun third-rate ship of the line built in 1666 and burned in 1668.

- The fifth Defiance was a sloop in service between 1671 and 1678.

- The sixth Defiance was a 64-gun third-rate ship of the line, built in 1675 and broken up in 1749.

- The seventh Defiance was a 69-gun fourth-rate built in 1744 and sold in 1766.

- The eighth Defiance was a sloop built at Bombay in 1766.

- The ninth Defiance was a 64-gun third-rate built in 1772 and wrecked in 1780 off the Savannah River.

- The tenth Defiance was a third-rate of 74 guns. She fought at the battle of Trafalgar and was broken up in 1817.

- The eleventh Defiance was a 4-gun gunboat built in 1794 and sold in 1797.

The twelfth Defiance was a 91-gun screw wooden ship, launched at Pembroke Dock in 1861. She was converted to a school-ship at Devonport in 1885, and taken to a berth off Wearde Quay in 1886. She was removed in 1930 and sold to ship-breakers in 1931. The Defiance was a steam two-line-of battle ship. Her tonnage was 3,475 and her length was 246 ft and her beam was 55 ft with the draught 24 ft.

The machinery was 800 nhp (Maudsley) and her speed not masted or stored was 11.884 knots. Trials were carried out in the Plymouth waters during February 1862.

The masts measured, Main 67 ft x 40 in. Fore 61 ft x 37in. Mizzen 51 ft 6 in x 27 in.

The cost of her construction was £119,442. If she had been armed and brought into normal naval service, her complement would have been 860.

HMS Defiance was laid down 20th September 1858 and launched 27th March 1861. She was sold to 'Castles', Passage Wharf, Plymouth, 26th June 1931.

Wearde Camp and Ministry of Pensions Hospital, Saltash

At the outbreak of the First World War, the 3rd Battalion of the King's Own Royal Lancaster Regiment was stationed in the fields between Cross Park and Wearde Farm. In the area which today is Broad Walk and the adjoining roads.

Their encampment comprised hundreds of tents, but plans were made for permanent quarters, wooden huts resting on concrete foundations, to be erected immediately to the south of today's Saltash Community School.

Over 2000 tons of stone for this work were supplied by Messrs Jefford's quarry at Tor, Burraton Coombe, between October 1914 and April 1915, with a further 900 tons to improve the access roads.

The contractor selected to undertake the construction of the camp was Carkeek of Plymouth, who, in 1916 faced a court action brought by St. Germans Rural District Council to recover the cost of damage to the highway caused by Jefford's steam wagon in transporting stone to the site.

'C' Company of the 4th East Surrey Regiment was also stationed at Wearde. In 1917 Field Marshall Viscount French who had commanded the British Expeditionary Force in France visited the camp to inspect the troops.

The enormous toll of casualties on the Western Front eventually changed the role of the Wearde encampment from a military base to a hospital for the wounded, and in 1920 it became the Queen Alexandra Convalescent Centre under the auspices of the Ministry of Pensions, with the patients being dressed in light blue clothing.

The people of Saltash were greatly supportive of the service men during the war and later of the hospital patients and events were organised for them. A report in the Saltash Gazette describes a social evening at the Church Rooms, attended by seventy convalescent men from the camp.

In 1921 it was reported that the Wearde Camp Amateur Dramatic Society gave a performance in the Wearde Camp Cinema. The hospital became redundant and the huts were removed during 1927-28. One of them was erected for the community at St. Stephens village and known as St Stephens Hall.

Where the camp once stood is now grass land, and nothing remains of the buildings which so many military personnel left to fight on the Western Front and to which some returned to recuperate from their traumatic experiences.

Courtesy Saltash Heritage

Familiar sights around Saltash were the men in light blue suits. They were accommodated at Wearde Camp being hospitalised as a result of injuries in World War 1, there were some who had suffered the gas attacks on the Western Front. My Father had a job in the camp and I used to visit it frequently and made friends with some of them. One tragic case that I remember was a character called 'Barney'. He had been gassed at **Ypres** in Belgium. It affected his mind and he would become violent and required restraining, he suffered fits which was rather frightening; however he was a good artist and constructed things and sort of adopted me as an end product for some original and unusual toys. We struck up a long friendship and hopefully it helped with his rehabilitation as he gradually improved. From any scrap he produced a magic lantern complete with hand-painted slides, which triggered an interest in photography which has never left me.

Norman Ash, a personal reflection

Acknowledging Norman's reflection on Ypres (above) I too have had the humbling experience of being a member of a band and marching many times on Armistice Day through the narrow streets of **Ypres** and under the Menin Gate. Visiting the War Graves within the Ypres salient and where the first gas attacks took place just past Hellfire Corner, there the Canadians suffered their first casualties. If you ever visit Ypres, a beautiful old town rebuilt from the ashes of war, you may be overwhelmed with the suffering that happened there and stretched beyond and across the Western Front.

Author John Hooper

The Dining Hall looking very regimental.

PHOTO'S COURTESY RICHARD PAYNTER

The huts above the road, is now the site of *saltash.net community school.*

The Ministry of Pensions Hospital, Wearde, Saltash.
The photographs record how well maintained the buildings and the grounds were kept.

Courtesy Richard Paynter and The Author's Collection

NAVAL REFLECTIONS

On a trip up the Lynher we would pass the naval training ship HMS Defiance, an old wooden wall. (The 'wooden wall' was the colloquial name for the Navy's Battleships before the days of Iron Clads). Two other ships became part of the facility with HMS Spartan providing a power plant and HMS Inconstant providing living quarters.

The economy of Saltash was boosted by the presence of Defiance. As a child I went to parties with the Cubs. My father served on her before WW1, my uncle was the blacksmith and after Defiance was relocated to Wilcove, Torpoint, my cousin George Tate and I joined her as Ship's Company in 1936.

At Wearde Quay when excise men were present a flag was flown to warn intending smugglers of their presence, a similar arrangement at the jetty, Charlotte Penna who lived on the pier, would drape an apron out of the window. Her efforts rewarded by grateful sailors. I joined up on June 15th 1936 as an Assistant Cook, much to my father's disgust. I then spent 32 happy years in the Royal Navy.

Courtesy Lt. Norman Ash RN Rtd. From his book Saltash & Naval Reflections.

Distribution of the messes was made up in multiples of eight to sixteen etc. A ration of butter per man was two and a half ounces a day, for a mess of 16 it would have been two and a half pounds per day.

After training at cookery school I was assigned to Defiance, Wilcove, Torpoint as a cook. Ratings were detailed for cooking duties and some bloomers coloured their abilities. Cabbage soaked overnight with soda, marrow fat peas not soaked, pastry similar to cement and dumplings that sank to the bottom of the pot. Our wages were 30 shillings (£1.50) a week and we put 6d (2½p) into a kitty as all mistakes had to be paid for.

Anecdote Norman Ash

Norman is a modest man but I would wish to add that he was on HMS Warwick when she was attacked and sunk off Trevose Head, North Cornwall from a torpedo attack by the German Submarine U-413 on the 20th February 1944 with the loss of 66 crew.

ECLIPSE OF THE SUN
30th AUGUST 1905

A postcard produced possibly for the crew of HMS Defiance showing from 12.30 p.m. onwards the eclipse of the Sun on the 30th August 1905 at Wearde, Saltash. I would imagine that a naval photographer would have photographed the eclipse.

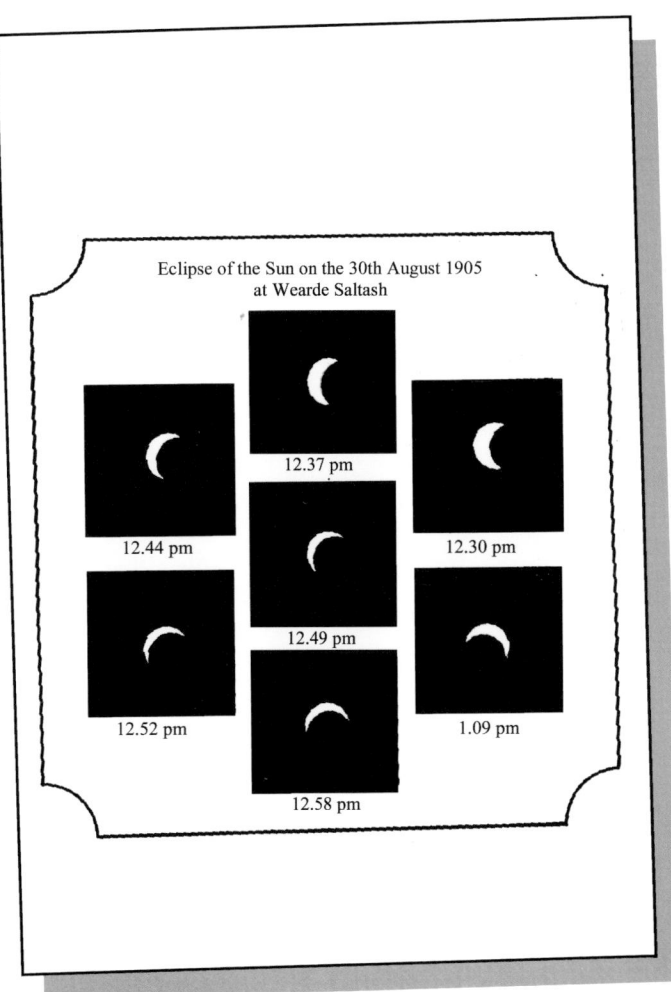

THE AUTHOR'S COLLECTION

The Figurehead HMS Defiance.

Courtesy of Her Majesty's Naval Base, Devonport Museum.

The figurehead was removed before the vessel was sold to Messrs Castle. Subsequently it was erected on the quarterdeck of the new *Defiance* at Wilcove. It was again saved when that vessel was scrapped in (or just after) 1955. The title *HMS Defiance* was revived at Devonport in 1972, when the depot ship HMS Forth was renamed *Defiance* and became the base ship for the Fleet Maintenance Group and the Second Submarine Squadron. In 1978 the base was transferred to new buildings ashore, and the figurehead was then mounted on the exterior wall of the main block. In 1994 HMS Defiance was axed as part of a major shake-up, and was absorbed into HMS Drake. The figurehead is now in the Dockyard Museum.

The origins of ships figureheads began in the early days of seafaring. They were used as religious symbols to protect the ship, and to express the sailor's belief that the ship was a living thing. They also believed that a ship should find its own way, and could only do so if it had eyes.

The size of some figureheads created weight problems, especially as they were made from hard woods; in the 17th Century, they were made predominantly from elm, this was changed in the early and middle of the 18th Century to oak. After an order by the Navy Board in 1742, figureheads were made from soft woods, such as pine. However, deal and teak were also used which proved to be more resistant to wood-boring insects and decay.

I would like to thank David Scoble of Saltash, a 'volunteer' for escorting me around the Museum and I would fully recommend a visit for anyone who may be interested in the amazing history and artefacts that the Museum displays. The Museum Group Visits Office can be contacted by telephone, 01752 554200.

THE LAST JOURNEY TO PASSAGE WHARF

Defiance was removed from Wearde Quay in October 1930 and taken to No.3 Basin in the Dockyard (near Flagstaff Steps), where for some months she (and the other hulks) continued in service while the new site near Wilcove was prepared.

When the *Defiance* was taken to her last resting place in June 1931, Messrs Castle at Passage Wharf, Cattedown, Plymouth, salvaged the seasoned timber and it was made into garden furniture, period reproductions in oak, teak, mahogany and half timbering for Tudor buildings. Also over a long period Castles' took to pieces the 'Ganges', 'Spartan' and the 'Cleopatra'.

In St Nicholas and St Faith Church, Saltash, there was an oak communion step (recently replaced) made from the timbers of HMS Defiance, also in St Stephens Church Saltash in 1934 the ceilings were renewed and the roof was repaired using teak wood from HMS Defiance.

Take a walk through the scenic nature reserve, Churchtown Farm, which overlooks the picturesque River Lynher, listen to the breeze and imagine the stories that could be related to a past era when the economy of Saltash was well supported by the activities on and off the river. Now we have important Industry on the other side of town with the Tamar Road Bridge that thousands of commuters a day cross to journey into Cornwall. In the last century Saltash had a ferry, a busy rail station, quaint shops with character, and numerous tea gardens where visitors purchased postcards and wrote on them "Having a nice time, see you soon". Progress and a new century have marked many changes; however, they have left behind treasured memories for us all to reflect upon.

*When I was a lad I served a term
As office boy to an Attorney's firm.
I cleaned the windows and I swept the floor,
And I polished up the handle of the big front door.
I polished up that handle so carefullee
That now I am the ruler of the Queen's Navee!*
Gilbert, HMS Pinafore

Castles' DESIGN CRAFTSMANSHIP

ARE YOU SITTING ON A PIECE OF THE 'DEFIANCE'?

"DEFIANCE"
A very sturdy chair
With 5" wide arms
Width between arms
1' 7"
Height of back rail 2' 9½"

S E A T S
Pleasant to look upon
Comfortable to sit on
Constructed for durability

PICTURES FROM A 'CASTLES' BROCHURE COURTESY BOB TAIT FORMER M.D. 'CASTLES'.

Now in the 21st Century - In our everyday lives of - the telephone, computers, laptops, mobile phones, the compact disk, digitals, the radio, television and films, the car, the aeroplane, satellites and space travel, all of which we take for granted. The *most* far-reaching in achievement and existence must surely be the radio. So, while we acclaim the early pioneers and geniuses; continuing research has revealed that their great work and determination was only the beginning of a science with endless technical possibilities. I hope my book reminds us of our outstanding innovators, like Captain Jackson and his contemporaries, and go some to way to celebrate their achievements, and to pay tribute to them all.